Praise for:

The College to Career Road Map:
A Four-Year Guide to Finding Your Path

"So many students drift through college aimlessly, only to panic near the end of senior year—with the real world quickly approaching! By providing a specific and detailed roster of experiences and action items students should check off during each of their four years in school, *The College to Career Road Map* affords them the opportunity to hone their talents, build their skillsets, take advantage of available resources, and focus on the small but critical steps that lead to an intelligent career decision. Savvy parents will make sure their students have this one on their bookshelves."

ALEXANDRA LEVIT
Author of *They Don't Teach Corporate in College:*
A Twenty-Something's Guide to the Business World (Career Press, 2004)
www.alexandralevit.com

"This book does an excellent job of helping students find a balance between practical concerns and pursuing their professional passions. The authors provide such thorough advice that I challenge the reader to find something they left out."

DR. JANIS BRODY
Author of *Bringing Home the Laundry: Effective Parenting for College and Beyond* (Taylor Publishing, 2001)
www.janisbrody.com

"The most detailed and easy-to-use guide to college and career preparation I've seen. The authors get it right: Not only will students who use *The College to Career Road Map* leave college with the skills and connections to start their careers, but—most importantly—they will also have found ways to connect career to their life's purpose."

BETH FEINE
Assistant Director of Career Services
St. John's University
Personal and Career Coach
Life Unbounded
www.lifeunbounded.com

"The *College to Career Road Map* is brimming with knowledge and vision. Every section invites students to consider their passions, innate talents, and what matters most as they embark upon their paths through each year of college. The writers have drawn from decades of experience to enumerate invaluable resources, opportunities, and strategies for success along the way. This book is a sensible companion (or requirement!) for freshman seminars. I will highly recommend it to my students."

MARY BURMASTER
Adjunct Instructor
Minneapolis Community & Technical College
www.minneapolis.edu

the

COLLEGE
to
CAREER
ROAD MAP

a four-year guide
to finding your path

·STUDENT EDITION·

TERESE COREY BLANCK, PETER VOGT
and JUDITH ANDERSON

Atwood Publishing • *Madison, WI*

The College to Career Road Map: A Four-Year Guide to Finding Your Path
by Terese Corey Blanck, Peter Vogt, and Judith Anderson

Copyright © 2006
Atwood Publishing
Madison, WI 53704

Cover and text design © TLC Graphics, *www.TLCGraphics.com*

Library of Congress Cataloging-in-Publication Data

Blanck, Terese Corey, 1961-

   The college to career road map : a four-year guide to finding your path
   / by Terese Corey Blanck, Peter Vogt, and Judith Anderson. —Student ed.
       p. cm.
   Companion to: The college to career road map : a four-year guide to
coaching your student.
   ISBN-13: 978-1-891859-66-3 (pbk.)
   1. College majors—United States. 2. College students—Vocational
guidance—United States. 3. College student orientation—United States.
4. Career development—United States. I. Vogt, Peter, 1967- II.
Anderson, Judith, 1971- III. Title.

   LB2361.5.B575 2006
   378.1'98–dc22

                                    2006025957

the

COLLEGE
to
CAREER
ROAD MAP

*a four-year guide
to finding your path*

Foreword

With college costing of up to forty thousand dollars annually, students simply cannot afford to drift haphazardly through four or more years of school. Fond memories of ivy-covered walls and late-into-the-night debates of esoteric issues won't cover the rent, student loan payments, or a car loan. Boiled down to stark post-graduation reality, your college education is an investment. The question you must ask yourself on Day One is, "Am *I* doing everything *I* can to maximize *my* return on *my* college education investment?" If you're reading this Foreword, I offer you my congratulations—you are embracing reality and are willing to engage in the strategic planning necessary to make your college investment a success.

As President and Founder of Internet career site CollegeRecruiter.com, I interact daily with college students and recent college graduates as well as the employers who want to hire them. While the job hunters fall into numerous, often changing categories, one clear dichotomy remains constant: There are those who have planned to get what they want and those who will take what they can get. So how do you become a part of the "conscious," as opposed to the "clueless"? Simple. You strategize, implement, evaluate, modify as necessary, and march forward. In other words, you take to heart the teachings of *The College to Career Road Map: A Four-Year Guide to Finding Your Path*.

The College to Career Road Map is not another "how to" book. Rather, it is an explorative journey—a trek designed to help you find *your* passion. The importance of the role of passion cannot be overstated. What could be more satisfying than preparing yourself to do what you're passionate about? The authors of *The College to Career Road Map* recognize this timeless truth and challenge you to engage in the introspective analysis necessary to uncover what that passion is.

Every journey begins with a first step. By embracing the teachings of *The College to Career Road Map: A Four-Year Guide to Finding Your Path*, you are enhancing the quality of your journey. May you discover your passion now so that you may live it in the future.

~ STEVEN ROTHBERG • 2006
Founder
CollegeRecruiter.com
www.collegerecruiter.com

• S T U D E N T   G U I D E •

Acknowledgments

The three of us would like to collectively thank all the people who have contributed to the process of developing this book in some way, shape, or form.

First, our gratitude goes to Marjorie Savage—author of *You're on Your Own (but I'm Here If You Need Me): Mentoring Your Child During the College Years* (Fireside, 2003) and director of the University of Minnesota Parent Program—who provided us with instrumental feedback and ideas regarding publishing. Her willingness to answer questions along the way has been essential to our learning process.

Our thanks to those who reviewed early drafts of the book. Among them are Scott Simpson and Kimberly Strauss-Johnson, who both reviewed the book in its early stages from a career development perspective. We would also like to thank several other early reviewers whose comments helped shape the content of the book: Bethany (senior at The College of St. Catherine), Brent (sophomore at St. John's University), and Lisa Fenhaus (parent);

Cindy Nelson (parent); Beth Feine; and Kathy Frost. Thanks as well to Gretchen Helmer for additional thoughts on wording and phrasing.

We also greatly appreciate the efforts and insights of our prepublication reviewers: Jeffrey Arnett, Janis Brody, Karen Levin Coburn, Rich Feller, Allison Hemming, Helen Johnson, Bill Krocak, Alexandra Levit, Robin Raskin, and Stephen Viscusi. Additionally, we'd like to thank Steven Rothberg and Jim Boyle for graciously writing the forewords for each of *The College to Career Road Map* books.

Another thank you to our spouses, who by proximity were called upon for their individual talent and expertise: Russell Blanck for his legal counsel and wording and phrasing advice; Lois Vogt for her willingness to do any and all research and administrative work; and Scott Anderson for his business perspective and technical assistance.

Finally, our heartfelt gratitude goes to Linda Babler, for seeing the value of offering parents and students a companion set of books. This approach goes beyond the normal bounds of the publishing industry. Thanks too to our editor, William Cody, who polished our words and made sure we were consistent. Additionally, Tami Dever and Erin Stark of TLC Graphics have been incredibly responsive to our ideas about the feel of the books, which was very important to us. Tami and Erin, your design has added a new dimension to the books and was a fun process to participate in—a tremendous bonus as far as we're concerned. To all three of you—thanks for bringing our books to life!

>—◦—>

My gratitude goes out to all those who have inspired me to find "what matters most" throughout my life. I can't imagine writing this book without the morsels of wisdom I received from those I met along the way.

Although high school wasn't the place I pondered my life path or even career, I must thank John Hegg for directing me to college. When I arrived at MSU Mankato's campus, my life's path began to take form. I met Arnie Oudenhoven, Sue Bartolutti, Tony Mueller—who always knew what I was going to say before I said it—and, in particular, Malcolm O'Sullivan. All of you shared with me the beauty of the "student affairs" profession, guiding students through the maze of the college experience.

I couldn't have wished for a more enlightening graduate learning experience than the one I found at Colorado State University. The insightful people there inspired me to question not less than everything I knew to be true. Dr. James Kuder, Dr. Dave McKelfresh, Rich Feller, and my classmates all challenged me to ponder the "big questions." Anne Williams Hudgens, I will never forget the horseback ride in the mountains above Boulder, where we pondered life and living intentionally. Your coaching touched my life and added meaning.

This book would never have happened without the love and support of my family and friends. My siblings, parents, grandparents, and Aunt Beverley provided the subtle nuances of family dynamics that played a vital role in nurturing out my true self. Mother, you generously partnered with me throughout my two years of writing. You have been my single most positive supporter. Thank you … your spirit is always welcome! I must mention my mother's dear friends in Canton, South Dakota, who were so much a part of anything good that became the children who've grown up there. I was fortunate enough to be one of them.

My heartfelt gratitude to the coffee shop crew: Caroline and Kelly, you always start my day right; and Jane … your enthusiasm and continued interest has been such great support … it was a pleasure to be greeted every time with genuine kindness! Thank you to Dr. Dave, Jeanine, and the LADC boys for listening to my updates. Lillian, you asked about the book every time I saw you and brought a smile to my face. Judy and Candace, you kept me balanced … thanks! My friends from the "Village," especially Tom and Jamie, thank you for asking and showing your excitement along my journey. Susan Ralles, without your question about how I knew all this college "stuff," … the parent book would never have been born … thank you. Clay, my kindred spirit in writing, your support of this project as well as your friendship over twenty years has been a true gem.

The many mentors, advisors, parents, friends, and family members I've been blessed to know along the way helped me find the path that resonated with me. My gratitude goes out to those who remain unnamed who served as mentors, guides, or friends.

A special tribute goes to my two partners, Peter and Judy, who've logged many hours with me, writing, laughing, and enjoying life!

I owe my deepest appreciation and gratitude to my husband. While I wrote this book with my co-authors, he bestowed upon me (us) his patience, humor, legal counsel, perspective, and interest. The courage he displayed in radically diverting from his own "pre-determined" career path is the fodder upon which this book is based! Your support of the book from conception has meant so much to me. Your belief in my work has been my strength. You are my true companion.

Last but not least, I dedicate this book to my lovely daughter, Alexandra Rachel Talia Corey Blanck, who inspires me to think about life and the tender parent–child connection that can let loose the possibilities of finding one's own soul. You are my teacher. I love you with all my heart. May you find the path that fits you throughout your life and may the journey be sweet.

~ Terese Corey Blanck

Any book you pick up is *much* more than its authors—and this book is no different.

I'd like to first thank my colleagues and co-authors, Terese Corey Blanck and Judy Anderson. Terese, I appreciate your visionary ideas and your passion. Judy, I appreciate your thoroughness and—especially—your closing abilities; *The College to Career Road Map* wouldn't exist without you.

Thanks as well to Linda Babler, publisher and president of Atwood Publishing. Linda, thanks for believing in both the concepts and the people behind *The College to Career Road Map*.

Thanks to my parents, Charles and Nancy Vogt, and my siblings—Kathy Frost, Mike Vogt, and Mark Vogt—and their families, who all have supported me in whatever I do. Thanks as well to my parents-in-law, Marilyn and the late Merv Gessele.

Many movie credits list the characters in order of their appearance in the film. My mind works that way when it comes to thanking people for their contributions to a book like this one. So from here on out, I'll start from the very beginning and work my way to the present. Here goes …

To my high school English instructor, Mark Hassenstab—I'm sorry for hassling you so much (it was the other boys' fault), but I appreciate your hanging in there with me and teaching me something about how to write. I still don't know why you never killed me or my partners in crime; thanks for your restraint.

To my Moorhead State University instructors Melva Moline and the late Joe Dill—thanks for teaching me to think before I write. And to Shelton Gunaratne—you drove me and my fellow students nuts with your nit-pickiness; but upon reflection, I can only thank you for refusing to lower your high standards. I now know that the power of the written word was at stake.

To my old colleagues at *The Forum* in Fargo, North Dakota—especially Mark Hvidsten (the guy who taught me the day-to-day ropes) and Dennis Doeden (the guy who hired me). I may not have become a sportswriter, but that doesn't mean I didn't learn a lot from you.

To my colleagues at Magna Publications in Madison, Wisconsin—Mary Lou Santovec, Charles Bryan, Doris Green, Robert Magnan, Linda Babler, and Marilyn Annucci. I appreciate your taking a chance on a fresh-grad rookie. And to you especially, Bob—thanks for teaching me how to actually think, whether it was over my keyboard or sitting across from you at Rocky Rococo.

To my graduate school professors at the University of Wisconsin–Whitewater, especially Anene Okocha. Anene, I appreciate all you taught me, not only about career development but also about research. Brenda O'Beirne, you modeled what it was like to be passionate about one's career—something I had honestly never seen before—and Steven Friedman, you made the idea of conducting research somehow appealing. Thanks to all three of you for the expertise you lent during the challenging journey that is called the master's thesis.

To my colleagues and mentors at the University of Wisconsin–Whitewater Office of Career Services—Gail Fox, Carolyn Gorby, Jerry McDonald, and Kathy Craney—as well as Marge O'Leary, Eunice Lehner, Margaret Pelischek, and Kris Fantetti. How can I ever thank you all enough for what you taught me about the field of career services? Gail, a very special thank-you to you—not only for inviting me into the field of career development but also encouraging me to stick around for a while. There's a book out there called *The Five People You Meet in Heaven*, which suggests that when you get to heaven you'll be met by the five people in your life who had the most impact on you. I'm certain, Gail, that you'll be one of the five where my life is concerned.

To my colleagues and mentors at Edgewood College Career & Counseling Services—George Heideman, Shawn Johnson Williams, Janet Billerbeck, Merle Bailey, Sharon Boeder, Rose White, and Julie Bonk. I couldn't have been more welcomed or more blessed. George and Shawn, special thanks to both of you for not only teaching me about career issues, but helping me understand that I had knowledge and skills to contribute too. Thanks as well to several other Edgewood colleagues and friends who taught me so much: Jan Zimmerman, Maggie Balistreri-Clarke, Maureen McDonnell, Todd Benson, and Debora Barrera-Pontillo.

I highly value my connection with the good folks at Monster and MonsterTRAK! Thanks in particular to the fabulous content producers I've worked with over the years: Denis Gaynor, David Long, Kristy Meghreblian, Christina Lopez, Christine Stavrou, Ryck Lent, Christine DellaMonaca, Ann Pariani, Norma Mushkat Gaffin, and Thad Peterson.

Special thanks to Barbara Winter as well. Barbara, I'll never forget the key piece of wisdom you shared with me over coffee a while back: "Writing, Peter, involves putting words on paper!"

Last but certainly not least, thanks to my wife Lois (for your patience even when you didn't always know what I was up to!) and my son Isaac (for letting me write even when you didn't always want me to). What would I do without my wonderful family? You're the reason I do what I do.

~ Peter Vogt

Many authors will say that writing a book is truly a journey—and this journey started long ago as I discovered my passion.

I'd first like to thank my partners, Terese Corey Blanck and Peter Vogt, who accepted the challenge of co-writing with open hearts and minds. I am truly amazed at how well each of our talents blended together to produce a book that will impact so many college students.

Thanks as well to my parents, Carol and Bill Roche, and my siblings—Nancy, Sandra (Nick), Stephen (Kristin), Charlie, and Helen—who will always be a part of my life. My in-laws, Jonette and Terry Anderson, and my sister-in-law Christi (Matt) also deserve a thank you for their love and support.

My thanks to Phil Fishman, adjunct professor at the University of Minnesota—who invited our class out for coffee and offered his interest and advice. This made a big difference to me. He guided me through the graduate school decision-making process and always takes my phone call at his law office. Terese Corey Blanck (yes, the same one) also spent many hours talking, teaching, and questioning during my four years in Comstock Hall. She too deserves much credit and thanks for introducing me to my career.

I also need to thank Orientation Services at the University of Iowa for shaping my entire graduate school experience. I was given a unique chance to be in a position of responsibility during my second year of graduate school. I want to thank Tom DePrenger, Jan Warren, Cathy Solow, Emil Rinderspacher, and Marilyn Kempnich for believing I could do the job. I also want to thank Cassidy Titcomb, Steve Hubbard, Dave Borgealt, and Laurie DuFoe for sharing all of what we learned during graduate school. I learned to expect more from college students than they expected from themselves and to share in their satisfaction when they reached those expectations.

I also want to thank Carmela Kranz, Elizabeth Patty, Karla Hoff, Libby Tate, and the late Deanna Hamilton for what they taught me at the University of Minnesota Alumni Association—and for the fun! The mentor program coordinators and alumni volunteers are too many to name—but you know how important the University of Minnesota Mentor Connection was to me. The Student Alumni Leaders were more than just a student group—I thank each of them for sharing their stories with me.

I also want to thank Laura Coffin Koch and LeeAnn Melin, who have been my mentors and friends—your wisdom and advice means a lot to me.

I want to thank my husband (and best friend), Scott, who has been completely supportive during this process. He has never questioned why I have the need or passion to make a difference—he only supports it. I dedicate this book to my children, Maxwell, Madeline, and Jack, who make me laugh every day as they truly explore their talents, passions, and values as only little children can do. It's amazing to watch each of your personalities take shape and to dream the dream of your future! Each one of you is special and will find your passion as only you can.

~ *Judith Anderson*

• STUDENT GUIDE •

Table of Contents

━◆━

━◆━

Introduction

This Book Is for You—the College Student!

As one of millions of college students today—or as someone who will soon join that bunch—you're under unprecedented pressure to succeed. After all, college is an enormous investment of not only your money, but your time and energy as well.

And then, of course, everyone around you expects you to have a *plan!* Ugh.

Creating and implementing a sensible yet exciting plan for college and future career success is a daunting task ... at best. What should you include in *your* plan? What are the most critical activities you need to pursue, and how do you prioritize them in a way that won't simply paralyze you?

The College to Career Road Map answers these questions and many more.

We wrote this book to make your college experience and your career development process an exciting, practical educational journey rather an overwhelming, boring chore. We want you to succeed and to feel good about the choices you make during your four (or more) years in college—not to mention your initial years in The Real World.

This book makes your journey from college to work more focused, intentional, and purposeful so that you find a rewarding, fulfilling career that fits *your* unique passions and innate talents—and that meets *your* definition of success, whatever success looks like for you.

In these pages, you'll discover specific academic and experiential activities you can pursue—during each of your years in school—to give yourself the best chance of landing a great job after you graduate. By completing these activities and, as importantly, reflecting upon them (with a little help from us ... more on that in a minute), you'll develop a "road map" of sorts for your future career, uncover opportunities and possibilities you've never thought about before, and even reduce your stress.

A Directive Guide to Finding Your Path

This book is a *directive guide* ... one that offers *specific expert advice* on how to identify—and eventually pursue—the career path that fits you best at this time in your life. By making this book a part of your daily life in college, you'll learn a process of introspection, exploration, and action that you'll be able to use the rest of your professional life. (Important note: Don't even bother thinking in overwhelming terms like "What am I going to do with the rest of my life?!" Chances are you won't do any one thing for the rest of your life.)

By the time you've finished reading this book, you'll see the connections among continuous learning, personal reflection, and experience—and how those connections give you insight into what really matters to *you* so that *you* can make *your own* decisions with *your own* direction. Think of this book as a helpful (though not perfect ... nothing is) recipe for college and career success and satisfaction.

Why Bother with All of This?

"Isn't this all just a little bit of overkill?" you might reasonably ask.

Not really. Obviously, we can't plan for *everything* in our lives—nor would we want to. But if you're like the typical college student, you'll be investing at least four years of your life ... and four years of your energy ... and four years of your hard-earned (or hard-borrowed!) cash in college, in hopes of recouping a substantial return on that investment over the course of your working life.

So doesn't it make sense to have at least a general idea of which career development activities you should be pursuing during college, and when? Of course it does—especially when you think about the specific rewards you'll reap:

- You'll be one of the comparatively few students who actually *graduates* from college instead of merely taking a few courses.

- You'll find a great career that aligns well with your passions, innate talents, and what matters most to you (i.e., your values).

- You won't have to move back home with Mom and Dad because you'll be well prepared, confident, and excited about your future.

All of this from a straightforward plan of action you can follow every semester of your college career.

How to Use This Book Effectively

Our four-year guide features specific action items for you to complete during your freshman, sophomore, junior, and senior years. Be sure to prioritize these tasks in order of their importance to *you* and then complete the ones that make the most sense to *you*. (It's beneficial if you do them all, but it's not required.)

As you go along, you'll notice that we ask lots of questions, which will then prompt you to jot down your *learning discoveries*—the important lessons you're learning about yourself and the world of work by engaging in each of the activities. (You'll be prompted with questions following each suggested activity.)

If you haven't noticed already, you'll soon discover that the book is broken down in a way you can readily understand—into your freshman, sophomore, junior, and senior years of college. Each of these sections then highlights the specific activities you can complete, academically and experientially, to explore your many career options and develop the skills you'll need for future success in the world of work.

Any career book you read will give you information and ideas. This book goes well beyond that to help you *act* on what you're learning. For only through taking action will you gain career direction.

We also tell you—specifically and plainly—*why* each activity is important and *how* to actually go about completing the activity. This isn't another book that simply tells you *what* to do and then cuts you loose.

We have a combined forty-plus years of experience working with college students and recent college graduates and helping them with their career-related struggles, in both the public and private sectors, in organizations large and small, and now in our own organization, College to Career, Inc. (www.collegetocareer.net). As importantly, we've all walked in your shoes ourselves. So we understand the challenges, the confusion, the excitement, and the frustration you face—all at once!—while you're trying to finish college and pursue your career ambitions.

We want to teach you what we've learned along the way and (hopefully!) help you avoid the mistakes we've made where our own respective careers are concerned. The first step—committing to reading and then completing the career-related activities that follow—is entirely up to you. But we absolutely, positively *know* you'll thank yourself later—many times over—for making that commitment right now and in the college years that are unfolding before you.

Let's begin.

Freshman Year

• FRESHMAN YEAR •

Exploration

Introduction

You've finally made it to campus! This is an exciting time of your life. It's your first opportunity to really *explore* the career and academic possibilities that are unfolding in front of you.

You have a lot of choices to make during this first year of school—in fact, during your first few *weeks*. These decisions will set the course for a successful first semester and first-year experience.

Paying attention to your academics is your top priority at this point. The expectations you're carrying from high school may or may not be in line with what your college/university is expecting of you now. So your best bet is to take charge of your course work from the beginning. Maybe you haven't ever mastered studying. Don't be afraid to brush up on your skills and ask for help (which, by the way, is almost always available right on campus). Your school wants you to succeed, so take advantage of the many resources it has to offer.

You'll also want to take a wide variety of courses so that you can begin exploring your interests and identifying possible majors. As you do, work hard to earn good grades, get to know your academic advisor and at least one of your professors, and start thinking about how your freshman year experiences will tie into your future career—because they will.

Academic Activities

Orientation

Attend orientation and register for your classes.

Why

Academic success actually starts before you officially arrive on campus. *Orientation* will be your foundation, for many reasons. You'll be given excellent academic information, you'll register for your first classes, you'll learn about campus resources, and you'll start to connect with people. You may even make your first friends. Your school knows what you and your fellow freshmen need to understand before you arrive on campus. So make sure you attend orientation!

How

1. You will have already received many mailings from the admissions and orientation departments at your school. You'll need to register for a particular orientation program in advance. Most schools expect you to attend a two-day program, and they often invite your parents to attend as well. If you haven't taken math and foreign language placement tests prior to attending orientation, expect to take them prior to registering for your first classes.

2. Attend orientation on the dates you registered for—more than likely sometime in June or July. Try not to put off attending orientation until just prior to classes starting; if you do, you'll be behind from the beginning.

• ROAD MAP QUESTIONS •

Passions: Are you passionate about attending the school you've chosen? Did orientation get you excited for your upcoming first semester?

_____

_____

_____

_____

Innate talents: During orientation, did you meet with an academic advisor that you can see yourself talking to for the next year to explore your academic/career strengths?

_____

_____

_____

_____

What matters most: Will this school be a place where you feel at home? Do you feel like you connected with a few people—students, faculty, staff—during orientation? Can you build relationships with some of these people over the next year or so?

_____

_____

_____

_____

_____

Core Courses

Use your required general education *core courses* to take a wide variety of classes, even in disciplines you're not familiar with.

Why

At most schools, you're required to take a certain number of *core courses*. These courses ensure (from the institution's perspective) that every student who graduates from your school has been generally exposed to a wide range of ideas—in the arts, the sciences, social issues, communication (written and oral), and other essential areas.

If you play your cards right, you can use your core course requirements to explore disciplines and the careers associated with those disciplines—because if you're like most college students (especially freshmen), you're aware of only a *tiny* fraction of the careers that exist in the world of work. (Did you know that there are more than twenty-thousand specific job titles out there, with the number growing every day?)

Remember: You weren't born passionate about whatever it is you're passionate about right now. Whether it's sports, music, writing, or something else, at some point you didn't *know* you enjoyed that activity so much; you had to expose yourself to it (or *be exposed* to it by someone or something else) before you were able to realize that you liked it!

Use this same experimental attitude in choosing your core courses. You may discover a passion you didn't even know you had—which may potentially become an integral part of your future career.

How

1. Set up a meeting with your assigned academic advisor shortly before you'll be registering for your courses for the upcoming semester. (You can set up this meeting via email, through a phone call, or by simply stopping by your advisor's office on campus.) Tell your advisor you want to discuss your course schedule for the upcoming semester—and that, in particular, you want to figure out how to take some classes that will let you explore careers/disciplines and meet your *core course* requirements at the same time.

2. Before meeting with your advisor, look at the schedule of courses for the upcoming semester. Talk with your friends and classmates about

some of the classes *they* have taken. Ask them what they liked about the classes and what they learned. Maybe one of these courses would intrigue you, too!

3. When you meet with your advisor, immediately reiterate one of your key goals: to take courses in a wide variety of disciplines while meeting your core course requirements at the same time.

4. Be open to courses your advisor suggests. After all, he/she probably knows the institution better than you do at this point. Tap that institutional expertise.

5. Don't be afraid to leave your meeting with your advisor *not* having decided on anything definite (yet). Give yourself a day or two to think about what you and your advisor discussed, and to do a little more research on certain courses you talked about, if necessary.

6. Come up with two or three versions of your course schedule for the upcoming semester, all of which meet your goal of diversifying the courses you take. As a freshman, you may not get your first-choice courses and/or schedule each semester. So have a Plan B and a Plan C that are equally acceptable—before you go to actually register.

7. Once you're in your new courses, don't be alarmed if you have an immediately *negative* reaction to at least one of them. After all, this may be a brand new topic for you, and it will be easy for you to be intimidated by it or bored with it. Give the course a chance instead of running out and immediately dropping it!

• ROAD MAP QUESTIONS •

Passions: What topics do you already enjoy studying? As importantly, what topics *might* you enjoy studying if you were to give them a chance?

_____

_____

_____

_____

Innate talents: In what academic areas do you already excel? And in which areas *might* you excel if you were to give them a try?

_____

_____

_____

_____

What matters most: Which subjects/disciplines matter most to you? Why? Which matter least? Why?

_____

_____

_____

_____

First-Year Experience Course

Take a *First-Year Experience* course offered by your school. (Note: These programs go by a number of names, including *University 101* courses, *freshman seminars, living/learning communities, courses in common,* and *block courses.*)

Why

Many schools offer their own variations of a *First-Year Experience* course. Some programs, typically called *University 101* introduce you to the campus and the resources available to you, and help you with the transition from high school to college. Other programs focus on academic experiences. Examples: *freshman seminar, courses in common,* and *block* courses.

You'll also want to see if your school offers *living/learning communities,* which allow students who are interested in the same areas of study to take courses together and live in the same residence hall/area.

All of these programs are designed to help you succeed academically as a freshman. Often, the courses are taught by tenured faculty members and give you a priceless experience that you would not have otherwise. This is especially important if you're attending a larger school, where you may find yourself in introductory classes that are as large as your entire high school class was!

How

1. You may receive information about *First-Year Experience* courses prior to orientation. But even if you don't, make sure to ask your assigned academic advisor (or another campus representative) about these types of opportunities while you're at orientation. You'll need to consider whether or not they fit with your academic plans, but usually there are options for most everyone.

2. Talk to any other students you know who attend your new school and participated in a *First-Year Experience* program. What do they have to say about the program? Most students don't regret being a part of something that was designed especially for them.

3. If you miss out on *First-Year Experience* opportunities during the fall, see if they're offered again during the spring semester. If they are, sign up!

• ROAD MAP QUESTIONS •

Passions: Do any of your *Freshman-Year Experience* courses appeal to your interests? What excites you about them? Do you enjoy working with other students?

_____

_____

_____

_____

_____

Innate talents: Are your professors and/or fellow students giving you any feedback on what you're good at? Are you surprised with what people are saying about your talents? Do you agree with their observations?

_____

_____

_____

_____

What matters most: Does learning in a community setting resonate with you? Why or why not?

_____

_____

_____

_____

_____

"How to Study" Courses

Enroll in a "how to study" course at your school so that you'll learn the skills that will help you earn better grades.

Why

Fairly or unfairly, grades are important to most of the employers you will one day pursue. For starters, if your grades are good, most employers will conclude that you've mastered essential workplace-related skills like how to organize and manage your time, how to do research and communicate well, and how to break down complex ideas into manageable bites of information that are easy to understand.

On a more immediately practical level, many employers make their decisions about whom to interview (and whom *not* to interview) for jobs and internships based on your cumulative grade-point average (GPA)—e.g., "We only interview students who have a 3.25 GPA or above." Fair? Of course not. But it's reality.

So if you get off to a bad start, grade-wise, during your freshman year, it can be very difficult (depending on just how bad you do) to recover from it and get your overall GPA to 3.0 or above (the minimum many employers will consider) by the time junior and senior year roll around.

How

1. Set up an appointment with the academic advisor who has been assigned to you by your school—that is, the person who helps you choose which courses to take each semester. (Depending on your school, this person will either be a full-time academic advisor or a member of the general faculty.) You can email him/her, call him/her, or simply stop by his/her office. Tell him/her that you're interested in learning about any programs or short courses your school offers on "how to study."

2. If your school has its own academic advising center, stop by there and ask one of the advisors if the center (or another department on campus) offers any programs or short courses on "how to study."

3. Once you've identified the "how to study" programs that are available on your campus, sign up for one of them and attend its meetings faith-

fully. Ask questions about things you don't understand (you will *not* be the only one!) and do your best to implement (in your classes) the academic strategies you're learning.

4. When the program you're taking ends, ask the instructor if it would be OK for you to contact him/her again in the future if you have other concerns. (Invariably, he/she will say yes!)

5. After you've been using some of your newfound academic strategies for, say, a semester, set up an appointment with the person who taught the study program you took and ask him/her to help you with anything you're still struggling with when it comes to your academics. No one expects you to master every new academic skill the first time!

• ROAD MAP QUESTIONS •

Passions: What academic *activities*—research, writing, reading, organizing—excite you the most? Which academic *subjects* excite you the most?

_____

_____

_____

_____

Innate talents: What study techniques come easily to you? Conversely, what areas will you need help with during your first semester?

_____

_____

_____

_____

What matters most: Does doing well in school matter to you? What priority do you place on getting good grades?

_____

_____

_____

Role of the Academic Advisor

Meet with your academic advisor at least twice each semester.

Why

At most schools, you're required to meet with your academic advisor only once each semester, and you _have_ to go to that meeting to get the formal institutional approval you need to register for your next semester's courses. If you set up and attend _another_ meeting with your academic advisor each semester, you can go beyond merely checking in and getting your advisor to sign off on your upcoming course schedule. Instead, you can talk about how your courses are going, what you're enjoying and not enjoying, what's going well for you academically, and what's not going so well.

It's the "not enjoying" and "not going so well" activities that are of greatest concern here. Your advisor can use this second meeting with you to point you toward resources, right on campus, that can help you address—and perhaps fix—whatever it is you're struggling with from an academic standpoint. The results will be better grades, higher satisfaction, and, as importantly, a boost in your confidence—all traits that are sought by the employers you'll be trying to impress not so long from now.

How

1. Set up an appointment with the academic advisor who has been assigned to you by your school. (You can email him/her, call him/her, or simply stop by his/her office.) Tell him/her that you're interested in meeting for a half-hour or so to talk about how your classes are going so far.

2. Before your meeting, write up a brief list of the things you'd like to talk about with your advisor. You might think in terms of four broad areas:

- Which courses you're doing well in so far, and why.
- Which courses you're struggling with, and why.
- Which courses you enjoy the most, and why.
- Which courses you enjoy the least, and why.

3. Type up your list of questions and bring them to the meeting. Bring a copy for your advisor as well so that he/she can look at the questions while you chat.

4. During your meeting with your advisor, stress that you're not demanding any magic answers or startling revelations (though you're always open to those!). Instead, simply say that you're taking stock of where you're at and that you're interested in any ideas he/she has for you. Then just let your meeting run its course. You never know what, if anything, is going to happen at a particular meeting. But it's almost impossible to leave a meeting with your advisor worse off than you were beforehand. (If this happens to you, however, don't be afraid to seek out a new advisor. Maybe the two of you just aren't clicking. That happens sometimes—just as it can in any human relationship.)

5. After your meeting, email your advisor a brief thank-you note for his/her time. You'll stand out in his/her mind for this seemingly simple act alone, thus improving your working relationship for the long term. You'll also get the chance to practice writing good thank-you notes—which will be essential when you're talking to employers about internships and jobs later in your college career.

• ROAD MAP QUESTIONS •

Passions: Did your advisor suggest any courses or strategies that (a) match your current interests, and/or (b) pique interests you didn't know you had?

_____

_____

_____

_____

Innate talents: Did your advisor suggest any courses or strategies that (a) match what you're already good at, and/or (b) reveal what you didn't _know_ you were good at?

_____

_____

_____

_____

What matters most: What patterns are starting to develop in your conversations with your advisor? Are you talking about how your academic plan will give you the life you want to live—whatever that means to you?

_____

_____

_____

_____

Meeting with Professors

Use the office hours offered by your professors at least one time per class during each semester.

Why

Research has shown time and again that the better you connect with your professors at college, the more likely you'll be to stay *in* college and finish your degree. Attending office hours is the easiest way to start building those connections. Often though, professors are working in their offices, they welcome interactions with students—like you!

Office hours offer you the opportunity to ask questions you may not feel comfortable asking in class. If you're struggling in a particular course, the professor can help you with learning strategies for that specific subject.

You'll be seeing your professors perhaps more than any other people on campus. Day in and day out, you'll be in their classes. It only makes sense, then, that the better you get to know them—and help them get to know you as a person—the greater the chance you'll be successful in college and the more they can help you.

But there's even more to the story. Later in your college career, when you're looking for an internship or even that first job after graduation, you're going to need a few *references*—people who can speak highly of you and your work. If you invest time and energy now in developing a good relationship with at least one professor, you'll have someone who is both willing and able to tell prospective employers good things about you.

Think about it this way: Which student will be most impressive to a prospective employer—one who merely *says* she has, for instance, strong research skills, or one whose English professor has *seen* those strong research skills in action and can thus tell employers of their authenticity?

How

1. Attend office hours at least one time for each class you're in during the semester.

2. Go to your meeting prepared to take the lead in your discussion with the professor. When he/she invariably asks, "So … what is it that you wanted to talk about?" you need to be ready to say something like this:

"I'm just interested in the things we're talking about in class. I'd like to learn more about them. Do you have any suggestions about books I could read or web sites I could visit that would cover more of the basics?" Then just see what your professor has to say.

3. If you're struggling in the class, be ready to share this information with the professor and ask for help.

4. Take a few notes on the professor's suggestions and be ready to answer questions that might come up during the discussion.

5. Keep an eye on the clock and take the initiative to wrap up your meeting when the allotted time has passed. Thank your professor for his/her time and follow up with a brief email reiterating your appreciation.

• ROAD MAP QUESTIONS •

Passions: Did your professor tell you about any resources, courses, or even careers that sound interesting to you? that you've never heard of before?

_____

_____

_____

Innate talents: Did your professor happen to point out to you that you're good at something related to the course—understanding the basic principles being discussed, for example, or developing and writing solid research papers?

_____

_____

_____

What matters most: Are there specific topics you like discussing with an expert (i.e., your professor)? What are they? Why are they so compelling to you?

_____

_____

_____

Investigating Potential Majors

Familiarize yourself with three to five possible majors at your school that *seem* to have the potential for matching your passions, innate talents, and values—that is, majors that are probably worth investigating in more depth. (No need to *choose* one yet, though! There's plenty of time for that later!)

Why

At most schools, you're going to have to decide on a *major* at some point—that is, the discipline to which you'll devote most of your academic time and energy. At most four-year institutions, you'll be required to declare a major once you've accumulated enough credits to be considered a junior—in other words, at or near the end of your sophomore year.

It's very easy to fall into the trap of thinking that if you don't choose the "right" major the first time, you're doomed. That is simply false. In fact, statistics show that many college students change their declared major at least once before they graduate, and some students change their major more than once.

But you can save yourself considerable time, energy, and perhaps even heartache later on by starting to fully explore majors *now*, during your freshman year. You can take your time to look around a bit, see what majors are out there and what they're about, and make an informed choice.

Think of it this way. If you were going to buy yourself a new outfit, wouldn't you be more likely to pick one you really like by starting early and studying as many options as you can—versus running into a store at

• FACT •

In the 2005 Graduating Student & Alumni Survey conducted by the National Association of Colleges and Employers (a trade organization made up of college/university career services professionals and employers who hire new college graduates):

- *More than 1 in 4 (26.5%) of the 750+ respondents said they had changed their major once during their college years.*

- *More than 1 in 10 (12.1%) said they had changed their major twice during their college years.*

- *Almost 1 in 10 (9%) said they had changed their major three times or more during their college years.*

the last minute and grabbing the first thing you see? The same logic applies to choosing a major.

This is a pretty critical decision, after all. As researchers from the Center for Labor Market Studies at Northeastern University have found (and written about in the *College Majors Handbook*—JIST Publishing, 2004), the typical employer is more interested in what you've majored in at school than what school you've attended.

So while the major you select isn't the be-all-end-all that will define your entire career, it *is* one of the more important decisions you'll make during your college years.

How

1. Find the online or printed version of your school's academic *catalog* (sometimes called *bulletin* or *course guide*). On your school's web site, you'll usually find this information under a broad section entitled "Academics" or "Programs and Majors." Conversely, you can usually find the printed version of your institution's academic catalog at the admissions office or campus-wide academic advising center.

2. Give yourself an hour or two to read through *all* of your school's academic majors and programs. Try as best you can not to rule out anything at this point—especially when it comes to your abilities (or lack thereof). For each program or major, ask yourself the following question: "My abilities aside, does this program/major sound *interesting* to me?"

3. Highlight each major that does sound interesting to you. (Remember: We're talking only about your *interest* at this point! For now, don't worry about whether you think you'd be any good at a particular major/program.)

4. Keep a separate list of majors you know nothing about. If, for a particular major, your honest answer

• FACT •

According to research by Northeastern University economists Paul Harrington, Neeta Fogg, and Thomas Harrington, it's one's college major—rather than the college or university one attends—that may just be the ticket into (or out of) a financially sound and rewarding professional life.

~ Northeastern University news release, August 5, 2004

to the question posed in No. 2 above is "I have no idea—I don't even know what this major *is*!", write that major down on this second list. (Note: Wouldn't it be tragic if you passed up on a potentially satisfying major because you said "no" to the question in No. 2 above when your response really should have been "I don't know"?)

5. Once you have your two lists completed—one of majors that sound interesting, the other of majors you honestly know nothing about— take the first list and, as best you can, prioritize which majors sound *most* interesting to you right now. Pick your "Top 5" as of now. These are the majors you'll use to *begin* your exploration.

6. On your second list, pick two majors at random and commit to at least reading a bit about them, at a minimum. Think of it like a trip to the antique store or the mall: Half the fun is just looking around at *all* the stuff, right?

7. Once you've finished your two lists, add to (or subtract from) them by:

- Talking to friends who are near the end of their college career and have already chosen a major. What do they like (or dislike) about their major? Why did they choose it?

- Talking with friends of your family who already have careers that interest you. What did they major in during college? What did they like (or dislike) about that major?

- Talking with your parents about their college majors if they attended college.

Remember: your goal at this point is not to decide what major to *choose*; for now, the idea is to simply decide what majors to *explore first!*

• ROAD MAP QUESTIONS •

Passions: What areas of interest have you always been drawn to? What did you dream about when you were little?

_____

_____

_____

_____

Innate talents: Have you been able to take classes to explore the things you're good at? Are you successful in these courses at the college level?

_____

_____

_____

_____

What matters most: Do you have a sense of your life's purpose at this point, or do you need to keep exploring the answer to this question?

_____

_____

_____

Value of International Study

Explore the possibility of studying abroad for a semester during your sophomore or junior year.

Why

A study abroad experience opens your eyes to a different culture and forces you to adapt to that culture very quickly—a skill that will be admired by the prospective employers of your future. Study abroad also teaches you unique skills and introduces you to what is becoming an increasingly global world economy and job market.

How

1. Ask your academic advisor or career counselor if your school has a Study Abroad office or department, or look for mentions of one on your school's web site and in your school's directory.

2. Call, email, or stop by the Study Abroad office and ask for general information on study abroad opportunities offered through your school. (You'll generally receive a brochure and some application materials, or perhaps a web site address to visit.)

3. Ask if you can meet individually with an advisor in the Study Abroad office, or if there are any upcoming introductory sessions for students like you who are interested in potentially studying abroad. If you can do either or both of these things, do so!

4. Ask your academic advisor, your professors, a campus career counselor (at your school's career center), and your friends if they know anyone

• FACT •

Study abroad does more than promote academic enrichment and personal growth. It also can enhance your employment prospects, especially in the fields of business, international affairs, and government service. Employers increasingly seek graduates who have studied abroad. They know that students who have successfully completed a study abroad program are likely to possess international knowledge and, often, second-language skills. Such students are also

likely to have other transnational competencies that graduate and professional schools and employers value just as highly: cross-cultural communication skills, analytical skills, an understanding of and familiarity with local customs and cultural contexts, flexibility, resilience, and the ability to adapt to new circumstances and deal constructively with differences.

~ Institute of International Education web site

who is currently studying abroad or who has done so in the past. Get the names and contact information of these students. Then contact them—in person or via phone or email—and ask them what studying abroad is really like. (Who better to tell you than students from your school who have done it?)

5. Visit the web sites of organizations like the Council on International Educational Exchange (www.ciee.org) and the Institute of International Education (www.iie.org) to learn more about study abroad possibilities.

• ROAD MAP QUESTIONS •

Passions: Have you ever dreamed about living in another country? Where? Do you know why?

_____

_____

_____

_____

_____

Innate talents: Could you adapt to a new environment and a different culture? Would you be comfortable if you didn't speak the language? Can you communicate in other ways?

_____

_____

_____

_____

What matters most: Is it important, in your mind, to learn about the world beyond the borders of the United States? Why?

_____

_____

_____

_____

_____

Experiential Activities

Living on Campus

Live on campus if at all possible.

Why

Living on campus will help you make friends, attend programs directed to your interests, and uncover ways to get involved. And involvement is the key to success at college.

You may have your roommate struggles and a small space to live in, but the memories of living on campus last a lifetime. You'll most likely meet your college friends—the ones you'll hang out with for the next few years (and, in a few cases, beyond)—during your first few weeks living on campus. Your life will be easier too, because meals will be prepared for you, you'll walk shorter distances to your classes, and you'll be surrounded by other freshmen who are experiencing the same things you are.

Remember, too, that one of the key traits future employers will be looking for is your ability to get along with other people. (On your second-grade report card, this was probably evaluated in a section called "works and plays well with others"!) By living on campus, you'll quickly run into people who come from all walks of life and have widely differing views of the world. You'll learn from them, and they from you.

How

1. Fill out your on-campus housing application the moment you get it in the mail in the months before your freshman year begins. Turn it in promptly along with any associated application fees. Living on campus is competitive at many schools when it comes to the particular residence hall you might want or the type of room you desire.

2. Get ready to meet your roommate. Your housing office will send you the name of your roommate sometime during the summer. Contact him/her prior to moving in to get to know him/her a bit—and to determine who's bringing what in terms of living possessions.

3. Keep an open mind where your roommate is concerned. You don't need to be best friends with him/her, but you'll have a much better year

if you find ways to get along. (And at the same time, you'll learn the key negotiating and problem-solving skills you'll eventually need in, say, an internship setting or your first-job workplace.)

• ROAD MAP QUESTIONS •

Passions: What are you learning about yourself by living on campus, and perhaps with someone new?

_____

_____

_____

Innate talents: What compliments are you receiving from your new college friends? Do they seem to be spotting in you skills and abilities you didn't even know you had?

_____

_____

_____

What matters most: What kind of people are you spending time with—especially if you're in your first few weeks of college? How are they influencing you and your decision making? Are you happy with how things are going so far? Are you being yourself or are you trying to be someone you're not?

_____

_____

_____

_____

"Welcome Week" Activities

Get involved at your new school by attending "Welcome Week" and convocation activities.

Why

Believe it or not, your school has been planning for you to arrive for more than a year. The people there have thought about how they can make you feel like part of the campus community, and they've planned a variety of "Welcome Week" activities for you and your fellow freshmen. Most importantly, events like convocation and other ceremonial activities initiate you into the academic traditions of your school. You won't want to miss the experience of being with your classmates as you are all formally welcomed to your school.

Your residence hall, the student union, student clubs, fraternities and sororities, and other campus organizations will also have activities offering the opportunity for you to get involved. Think about what you'd like to get involved with during your first semester. Pick something that's interesting to you—and that will teach you something helpful for your future career, if only on a small level.

How

1. Your school will give you information about student activities fairs, convocation, and similar events—starting at orientation. Watch for this information and attend the events that will motivate you and get you involved.

2. Grab a few of your new friends and get out of the residence hall during the first few days of school. Explore a bit.

3. Get advice about activities from your residence hall's *resident assistant* (RA) or *community advisor* (CA). He/she will have great tips about what activities are worth your time.

4. Choose one way to get involved and follow through with it.

• ROAD MAP QUESTIONS •

Passions: What special events did you attend during the opening days of school, and how did they make you feel? Are you excited about involving yourself in a particular organization that interests you? Are you going to join? When?

_____

_____

_____

_____

Innate talents: Throughout all of the activities you participated in, what felt easiest to you? Did you feel comfortable going alone? Did you prefer to bring a friend?

_____

_____

_____

_____

What matters most: Do you feel more connected now that you've found some options for campus involvement? Do you feel your school is a good fit for you? Why or why not?

_____

_____

_____

_____

Campus Organizations

Join at least one campus organization on campus.

Why

Year after year, when employers across the United States are surveyed about the key *soft skills* they look for as they consider college students for internships and jobs, they consistently give the highest rankings to strong communication skills, the ability to work well with other people in small groups or teams, demonstrated self-motivation and initiative, and proven leadership skills:

In the *Job Outlook 2005* survey—conducted by the National Association of Colleges and Employers (a trade association for college/university career services professionals and employers who hire new college graduates)— employers were asked to rank the importance of a variety of soft skills in new college graduates (with 5 being "extremely important" and 1 being "not important"). The top-rated skills (and their average scores):

Communication skills (written and verbal) 4.7

Honesty/integrity. 4.7

Interpersonal skills (relates well with others) 4.5

Strong work ethic 4.5

Teamwork skills (works well with others). 4.5

Analytical skills 4.4

Motivation/initiative 4.4

Flexibility/adaptability. 4.3

Computer skills. 4.2

Detail orientation. 4.1

Leadership skills 4.0

Organizational skills 4.0

What better way to show you have a few or all of these key characteristics—and then some—than to join and eventually get heavily involved in a campus organization? You may focus on one geared to a discipline or field that interests you or just one that fits a special interest, such as the ski club, your residence hall government, etc.

Employers aren't naive—they know the difference between the student who joined a campus organization last semester of *senior* year in an attempt to build his/her resumé and the student who joined a campus group *freshman* year and became an integral part of its ongoing success. One is a pretender; the other is the real deal.

In addition, feeling connected to your campus community and participating in campus activities will make you feel more at home. You'll be with people who have similar interests and who you'll easily click with.

How

1. Ask a few students you know (or your residence hall advisor if you live on campus) what student groups they're aware of and, especially, how you can find out about *all* of the existing student groups on campus.

2. If you're taking a class that is discussing topics of great interest to you, ask the professor if there are any campus organizations on campus that relate to the topics in question.

3. Go on your school's web site and look for a link to the Student Activities or Student Organizations office. (Alternatively, look for a mention of this office in your school's printed student handbook.) Someone on your campus has a complete list of *all* campus organizations at your school. Chances are, this is the office that has it.

4. If your school offers a Campus Involvement Fair or Student Activities Fair (typically at the beginning of the school year), be sure to attend. At this event, various campus organizations set up displays at tables so they can recruit other student members.

5. Once you've identified a few student groups that sound interesting, contact a student leader of each group via phone or email. Tell the person the group sounds interesting and that you'd like to learn more about it.

6. Attend a meeting or two of a few of the organizations that interest you most. Which groups seem to be thriving? Which ones aren't doing so well? Can you see yourself fitting in within one of these groups and perhaps even becoming a leader of that group someday?

7. Pick one group and become a consistent meeting attendee. If an opportunity comes along for you to volunteer in some small way, take advantage of it. Do *not*, however, take on so much that you end up overwhelmed! One or two quality experiences are much better than four or five unsatisfying, surface-level experiences.

• ROAD MAP QUESTIONS •

Passions: What activities do you like (or might you like if you tried them)? Why?

_____

_____

_____

_____

Innate talents: What are you good at doing, especially in a group setting? What skills—especially _soft skills_ (e.g., teamwork, communicating effectively)—are you obtaining or could you obtain in the campus organizations you're considering?

_____

_____

_____

_____

What matters most: What matters to you when it comes to how you spend your limited free time?

_____

_____

_____

_____

Volunteer Activities

Devote a little of your time and energy to participating in volunteer activities.

Why

Volunteering is a great way to introduce yourself to different career possibilities and settings, build your skills, and demonstrate your ability to manage your time and energy well. Plus, of course, volunteers are sorely needed in cities large and small across the entire United States.

There's another, intangible benefit to you as well: Most prospective employers will have profound respect for you if you've done volunteer work. Why? Because it shows you care about people beyond yourself and issues beyond those in your own daily life. It demonstrates that you're willing to help address problems—if only in a small way—instead of merely complaining about them.

Moreover, you'll find that many employers are involved in volunteer activities themselves. So you might well meet your future internship supervisor or employer while, for example, you're helping to build a Habitat for Humanity house or developing the new web site for a local nonprofit agency.

How

1. Many colleges and universities have a Service-Learning office or Volunteer Center (or similarly named office) that serves as a clearinghouse for volunteer opportunities in the local area. If your school has such a center (check the campus web site to find out, or ask your academic advisor and fellow students), stop by the facility sometime soon and see if there are any volunteer activities you could work on. Even if you're able to devote only an hour or two a month to volunteering, it will make a difference—to you and the people and organizations that need the help.

2. If your school doesn't have a Service-Learning office or Volunteer Center, check with the Student Activities office or Student Organizations office (or similarly named office) to see if it publicizes local volunteer opportunities.

3. In many larger cities, the United Way serves as the clearinghouse for most of the volunteer activities in the area. If you live in a decent-sized city, contact the local United Way to see if it can help you uncover vol-

unteer opportunities. (Be sure to visit the United Way web site at www.united-way.org.) You can also use the VolunteerMatch web site (www.volunteermatch.org) to search for volunteer opportunities in a given geographic area.

4. Check your local newspaper to see if it has a section called "Volunteers Needed" or something similar. (Many newspapers offer this service, for free, to help local organizations recruit volunteers.)

• R O A D   M A P   Q U E S T I O N S •

Passions: Is the volunteer activity you're involved in something you might like to do for a living someday? Why or why not?

_____

_____

_____

Innate talents: Are you good at the activities you're performing as a volunteer? Or could you be if you were to gain some more experience?

_____

_____

_____

What matters most: Does the cause behind each of your volunteer activities matter to you—so much so that you might want to make a career out of it someday? Why or why not?

_____

_____

_____

Part-Time Work

Find a part-time job, either on campus or off, if you've been successful academically. If you're struggling academically, you'll need to evaluate whether you can add this experience to your plate.

Why

Although your academics come first, the college students of yesteryear could often get by without picking up any job experience during college. Back then, a college degree was typically seen as enough—on its own—for a student or recent graduate to land an entry-level job.

Those days are gone—long gone. If you don't believe it, listen to the employers who are surveyed each year by the National Association of Colleges and Employers (a trade association for college/university career services professionals and employers who hire new college graduates).

In the *Job Outlook 2005* survey—conducted by the NACE—participating employers were asked to rank the importance of various types of work experience in new college graduates (with 5 being "extremely important" and 1 being "not important"). The top-rated experiences (and their average scores):

Relevant work experience 4.0
Internship experience 4.0
Any work experience. 3.5
Co-op experience 3.4

The *College Hiring 2005* survey of employers—conducted by online job site CareerBuilder.com—underscores the point. When the more than six hundred participating employers were asked about the top characteristics they look for when hiring new college graduates for full-time, permanent jobs, the No. 1 answer (cited by 28 percent of the respondents) was "relevant experience." (Coming in at a distant No. 2—cited by just 12 percent of the respondents—was "professionalism during the interview.")

If you put yourself in a future employer's shoes for a moment, you'll begin to understand why experience is so critical to them when they're evaluating college students and recent grads for jobs and internships. Bad hires cost a company thousands (or even millions, in the case of a large organization) of dollars a year. They also hurt company morale by frustrating the many *good* employees who are forced to work with less-than-ideal colleagues.

By picking up some hands-on work experience during college—starting your freshman year (if not before)—you show future prospective employers, first and foremost, that you're able to *handle* basic (and often assumed … foolishly!) job tasks like showing up, being responsible, and working well with other people. But perhaps more importantly, you'll develop new skills, get a better sense of what you like (and don't like!) about various work settings, and gather the evidence you'll need to *prove* to future employers that you can do what you're claiming you can do.

Of course, a little extra money in your pocket doesn't hurt either!

How

1. Look in the classified section of your school's student newspaper to check out part-time positions listed there. Many times the companies that advertise jobs in college newspapers are looking specifically for college students who have flexible schedules.

2. Go to your school's career center and see if it offers—in print form or online—a list of available part-time jobs in your city/area.

3. Many schools have a Student Employment Center (or similarly named office)—separate from the career center—whose sole purpose is helping students find part-time jobs. Does your school have such a resource? If so, be sure to tap it!

4. Check out the classified ads of your local off-campus newspaper (either in print or online). If you live in a large, urban area, be sure to use not only the daily newspaper classifieds but also the classifieds of the many suburban papers in the area. (Note: Practically all newspapers these days make their classified ads available both in print and online. So there's no need for you to go out and actually track down physical copies of the many suburban newspapers in your area.)

5. Does your city have a government-sponsored Workforce Center (or similarly named office)? If so, check out its web site for part-time job listings.

6. Ask a few of your fellow students about part-time jobs they're aware of. Are any of them working at places where they could help *you* get an interview for a job?

7. Do any of your professors know about part-time jobs in the area that might serve the dual purpose of helping you get some experience in a field that truly interests you? Ask them! They may have referred other students to these same organizations. Perhaps you'll be their next success story!

8. If your campus resources leave you dry, register with local staffing firms or temporary employment (*temp*) agencies to see what they have to offer. Temping is a great way to gain exposure to various industries and make a little money. Plus, these organizations generally love working with college students, whose schedules are typically more flexible than most.

• ROAD MAP QUESTIONS •

Passions: Might you want to work in the field/setting/industry where you've landed a part-time job? Or have you instead discovered that this is *not* the field/industry/setting for you?

_____

_____

_____

Innate talents: What do you do well in the part-time job you've landed? What specific skills are you gaining from it?

_____

_____

What matters most: Do the activities in your part-time job matter much to you, or are they merely "all in a day's work" as far as you're concerned?

_____

_____

The Career Portfolio

Start collecting items for the *career portfolio* you'll be building later on in your college career—the formal, three-ring binder that will feature, for instance, excellent papers you've written, brochures you've designed, awards you've won, research you've completed, and the like.

Why

Most employers have been burned a few times by people who have said (in an interview, for example) that they could or would do something but ultimately were unable to back up their words when they were on the job. The less-than-flattering term employers use for these people: "bad hires."

Employers, as you might imagine, don't want to make any bad hires. And so over time, they tend to become increasingly skeptical of the things they're told by job and internship seekers. They end up with an attitude that might be summarized—quite understandably—as "show me the proof!"

A *career portfolio* will give you the proof you need to back up your resumé and interview claims. Instead of merely *saying* to an employer, "I have strong communication skills" (to which an employer might mentally respond, "If I had a dime for every time I've heard that one!...") you'll be able to *prove* you have strong communication skills by turning in your portfolio to the fifteen-page research paper on which your instructor wrote, "One of the best-written papers I've read in some time. Outstanding job!"

Eventually, your career portfolio will emerge in the form of a nice three-ring binder. (Think of it as a scrapbook with a career emphasis!) For now, though, all you need to do is start *keeping* and *collecting* the materials that might one day appear in your portfolio. It's time to become a packrat!

How

1. Go to an office supply store and buy a large, plastic box with a cover. (It will cost you under $10.) Meet your "career portfolio box"!

2. Whenever you create or accomplish something that carries even the slightest hint of your abilities and/or interests, put some result of that creation or accomplishment into your career portfolio box. Example: You write a simple computer program for a basic programming course.

Print out the code and put it in your career portfolio box. Another example: Your picture appears in the school newspaper during Campus Cleanup Day in the spring. Cut out that picture, put it in a folder or some other protective covering, and save it in your career portfolio box.

3. If you're ever in doubt about whether to bother keeping something or not, keep it! It's far better to save too many materials than too few. And what might seem irrelevant or unimportant today could turn out to be quite crucial tomorrow. Save, save, save!

4. If you have the time and inclination, visit your school's career center and see if someone there can either show you an example of a completed career portfolio or refer you to books that describe the concept in detail (with examples).

• ROAD MAP QUESTIONS •

Passions: As you look through the materials you're collecting in your career portfolio box, do you see any patterns when it comes to what you enjoy doing? Were any of the experiences associated with the materials especially enjoyable for you? Why?

_____

_____

Innate talents: What do the materials you're collecting demonstrate about your skills and abilities? If you want to prove to a future employer that you have, for example, strong teamwork skills, do you have any portfolio evidence to back up that claim? If not, how can you get some?

_____

_____

> **What matters most:** What have you noticed in your collection of items that seems to be a repeating theme? Do you see any clues about what will be important to you in your future career?
>
> _____
>
> _____

Your Resumé

Write a first (and very rough!) draft of your resumé—knowing it will change considerably in the months and years to come.

Why

For better or worse, fairly or unfairly, prospective employers (for jobs and internships) will make their first judgments about you by reading (or ... gasp ... tossing!) your resumé. So it's got to be good. If it isn't, the employer will choose someone else to interview and, ultimately, hire.

Fortunately, your resumé doesn't have to be good _immediately_—i.e., right now, during your freshman year. In fact, you'll be the rare student indeed—freshman or not—if you put together an outstanding resumé on your first (or second or even third) attempt.

But none of that matters right now. All that matters is that you get something—anything—on paper. You can edit your resumé later, with the help of a career counselor at your school's career center, one or more of your favorite professors, your parents, or all of the above.

For now, you just have to start. Put some material to paper/screen, even if it's awful to begin with!

How

1. If you want to, try to write a draft resumé completely on your own at first. You can consult one of the dozens of resumé books on the market for ideas, or look for examples on the Internet.

2. Alternatively, you could work on your resumé with the help of a career counselor at your school's career center. In reality, there is _no_ need for you

to take on this important project all by yourself—especially when expert help is readily available at the campus career center. So if you prefer the collaborative approach to writing a first-draft resumé, this is the way to go.

3. You may not need to actually use your resumé until months down the road—which is nice, as you'll have plenty of time to revise it. If, however, you need a well-done resumé sooner versus later—to apply for a part-time job or an internship, for example—you'll need to take your completed first draft to a campus career counselor or another knowledgeable person (e.g., professor, parent, family friend) and have him/her help you improve it. Don't be surprised if it takes several attempts before everything is just so on your resumé. No one writes a perfect resumé in only one or two attempts!

4. As you write the various subsections of your resumé, try to focus not simply on *duties* or generic *activities* from your past (e.g., "made calls") but instead on *accomplishments* and *achievements* (e.g., "helped raise $1,200 for Habitat for Humanity via cold calling"). Your career counselor can teach you more about this important distinction.

5. If you're completely befuddled by this task, at least go online or to the campus career center to next start viewing some resumés to become familiar with what's typically included. This research will give you direction about what you need to do between now and next summer (or early sophomore year) to get your own resumé started.

• ROAD MAP QUESTIONS •

Passions: Does your first-draft resumé do a good job of showing the reader what some of your key interests are? If not, how can you improve it?

_____

_____

Innate talents: Does your first-draft resumé do an effective job of documenting—as completely as possible—the skills and abilities you've gained or used in your courses, student activities, jobs, and volunteer work? Does it help the eventual reader understand what you've *done* and what you *can do*?

_____

_____

_____

_____

What matters most: Have you highlighted accomplishments that are truly important to you, such as community service, volunteering, and other unique experiences that help define who you are?

_____

_____

_____

_____

The Campus Career Center

Visit your school's on-campus career center and learn about the available resources there.

Why

Practically every college/university in the United States has a career center. Whose money pays the bills for these career centers? Yours, in the form of your tuition and student fee dollars. (Note: Typically, the campus career center's services are free to you as a student. But just remember that these "free" services are the result, in part, of the not-so-free tuition and fees you pay your school each semester!)

Of course, the money is only part of the story (and a small one at that). Here are a few more practical reasons to tap the resources of your school's career center—starting freshman year:

- It offers print, online, and people resources that will help you more easily explore majors and careers.

- It has statistics on the types of jobs obtained by past students from your school in various majors—so that you can easily learn, for example, what types of jobs have been landed by sociology majors … or chemistry majors … or _____ majors from your institution.

- It's staffed by professionals whose essential purpose is to help you and your fellow students with complex career-related issues—through one-on-one counseling, courses, seminars, and computerized career guidance programs.

- It's where you'll eventually learn more about internship and co-op opportunities, perhaps interview for a post-graduation job, and do research on future educational endeavors like graduate or professional school.

How

1. Find the career center link on your school's web site. (Note: At your particular school, the career center might be called the Office of Career Services or the Career Development Center or the Career Management Center or something else with the term "career" in it.) Click through to the career center's home page so you can see where the facility is located and how to contact someone there.

2. Depending on your personal preference, call or email the career center—or simply stop by—and tell the person who responds that you're a freshman and you'd like to learn about the resources available to you.

3. You'll probably be asked to set up an appointment for a later date. Go ahead and do just that.

4. You may be asked if there is a particular counselor you'd like to see. If you honestly have no preference, go ahead and make an appointment with the person who is available the soonest. But if you *do* have a preference—someone who was very helpful to one of your friends, for example—don't be afraid to ask for that person by name, even if you have to wait a little longer. (Note: As is the case in any other business,

some of the people who work at the career center will be more helpful than others. If you can pick a helpful one the first time, so much the better!)

5. Go to your first meeting ready to start working on one goal: learning about available resources. It's perfectly all right for you to simply say to your counselor, "I'm ready to start exploring the resources you offer in order to consider a variety of majors. But I need some guidance on *how* to do all of that, starting now while I'm a freshman." The counselor will almost certainly see you as a refreshing change of pace from the steady stream of second-semester sophomores who show up an hour or two before they have to register for their junior-year courses and say, "Can you help me pick a major … by four o'clock this afternoon?!"

• ROAD MAP QUESTIONS •

Passions: At this point in your life, what activities might you enjoy if you were to give them a try? What topics might be interesting to study in depth? Have you considered taking an interest inventory to get some additional ideas?

Innate talents: What's your current sense of what you're good at? Have you ever thought about taking a timed abilities test to a) confirm what you already know you're good at, and b) uncover things you didn't know you were good at?

_____

_____

_____

_____

_____

What matters most: Right now, what matters most to you in your life? What might matter most to you in the future career you choose (e.g., how much money you make, the lifestyle you live, the type of setting you work in)? Have you considered completing a values inventory or talking with a career counselor to identify values-related themes in your life?

_____

_____

_____

_____

_____

_____

_____

_____

_____

Researching Careers

Begin researching careers of *potential* interest to you.

Why

Statistics show that there are more than twenty-thousand specific job titles in the United States! How many of these jobs do you honestly know anything about? How many of them are completely new to you?

If you're like most college students—and people in general, for that matter—you're trying to choose a career from a box of, at best, one hundred possibilities—leaving 19,900 (probably more!) beyond your awareness, let alone your thoughtful consideration. What if one of these other careers would be a great fit for you? What if you unknowingly pass it by?

That's why career exploration and research are so important.

Let's be clear: There's no way you're going to learn about the ins and outs of twenty thousand career possibilities. You'll be in college forever if you take that route! But wouldn't it be nice to go beyond the opposite, paltry extreme of only a hundred (or maybe far fewer!) possibilities? Wouldn't you like to make your choice from a larger "catalog" of options?

By completing some very basic career research activities, you'll be able to do just that.

How

1. Look for books about various careers. Begin your search by talking to a campus librarian and seeing if the school's library has career exploration books. As importantly, visit your school's career center and start looking through its library of books. Additionally, head for your local bookstore and spend some time in the "Careers" section, paging through career guides. You may not know it, but several publishers produce books in the *Careers in* _____ (e.g., *Careers in Marketing*) or *Careers for* _____ *Majors* (e.g., *Careers for Psychology Majors*) genre.

2. Ask your school's reference librarian to help you track down articles about careers of potential interest to you. Perhaps the local business newspaper did a story on nursing recently. Or maybe one of the thousands of *trade publications* in the United States recently ran a piece on career opportunities in biotechnology. A reference librarian can help you get your hands on the articles you want.

3. Look for web sites describing careers that interest you. The widely popular search engine Google (www.google.com) is a fabulous tool for this type of research. What kind of job can you get with a degree in finance? Try a Google search on the phrase "careers for finance majors" or "What can I do with a major in finance?"

4. Talk (in person or via phone or email) to people in careers of potential interest to you. For instance, if you read an article about someone in a profession that intrigues you, email that person and ask if you could talk to him/her about what he/she does. You'll be surprised by how willing most people are to tell you more about their jobs—in great part because most of us enjoy talking about ourselves!

5. Visit your school's career center and ask a counselor there to teach you ways to explore careers. Ask for different approaches you can use. If you enjoy talking to people in person, for instance, you might benefit from directly contacting a person in a field that interests you. Conversely, if you prefer learning by reading, you'll probably get more out of finding the right books, articles, or web sites describing the career you want to learn more about. Both of these approaches to career research are equally valid—and quite effective!

• ROAD MAP QUESTIONS •

Passions: What subject do you spend the most time talking about or reading about? What are its potential career possibilities?

_____

_____

_____

_____

_____

Innate talents: Where might you apply your best—and favorite!—abilities and skills in the world of work?

_____

_____

_____

_____

_____

_____

_____

What matters most: What can you envision yourself doing for forty (or more) hours a week? Does making a certain amount of money drive you? Do material possessions matter to you? Do you need to "make a difference" through your work?

_____

_____

_____

_____

_____

_____

_____

_____

_____

dreams ... discoveries ... reflections ...
intentions ... discussions

➤—◦—➤

Mapping Your Direction

Uncovering Your Purpose
Freshman Year

*"Having a purpose is the difference between
making a living and making a life."*

~ TOM THISS

Now that you've completed your freshman year and focused on *exploration*, you're probably beginning to know yourself in a whole new way. Take some time now to put this newfound wisdom together by writing what you know to be true regarding the following questions.

Use your responses to begin developing the bigger picture of your life— your *purpose*.

Purpose

The underlying theme of this book is centered on *purpose*. When you're truly clear about your life's purpose, you feel a sort of connectedness to greater meaning.

The questions that follow will help you begin to uncover your purpose. Take the time to thoughtfully ponder them—and the meaning of the answers that lie within you.

If you can articulate your purpose, what is it? If not, think about the last few times you experienced a wonderful mood or felt totally in sync with life. What you were doing when you felt this way? Were you helping or serving others? Were you creating something new or beautiful? Were you solving a problem? What insights have you gained about your purpose?

Here are two more purpose-related questions for you to contemplate right now:

- Am I on course with my purpose?
- Am I learning more about my purpose?

Dreams—Life's Destinations

Where is it that you want to go, with whom, and doing what at this time in your life? What kind of life do you want to be engaged in right now? Does it align with "what matters most" to you?

_____

_____

_____

_____

_____

_____

_____

_____

_____

_____

_____

_____

_____

_____

_____

_____

_____

_____

_____

Discoveries

Scenic highways: Write about the "scenic highways" of your freshman year—that is, what went well and the exciting events that spoke directly to your heart. What has been revealed to you about your abilities, skills, interests, and values? What has been revealed to you about who you're becoming?

_____

_____

_____

_____

_____

_____

Roadblocks and speed bumps: Write about the "roadblocks" and "speed bumps" you encountered this past year—your problems and struggles, big and small. How do they relate to your dreams and your future? What have you learned about yourself? Do you have any gut feelings about what it all means? What are these gut feelings?

_____

_____

_____

_____

_____

_____

Reflections

What are your deepest thoughts—the ones that are very personal and private? Take at least ten minutes to write freely about the dreams you currently have for your future.

Intentions

Set your course: What actions will you commit to that will move you toward your dreams? Reread the list of *academic* and *experiential* activities from freshman year and highlight the ones that are most important for you to act on. Do you need to set a deadline for when you want to have these tasks completed? If so, create a timeline below:

Document at least two commitments you're willing to make to yourself and think about the time it will take to actually complete these activities. Record the date you want each of them completed:

Commitment one: _____

Completion date:_____

Commitment two: _____

Completion date:_____

Daily intentions: What activities can you commit to each day to move your dreams ahead (e.g., attending classes, studying, talking with mentors, journaling your thoughts, reading through portions of your journal)?

_____

_____

_____

_____

_____

_____

_____

_____

Discussion and Dialogue

Creating your support system: Who in your life understands you best? Who supports you through thick and thin? With whom do you feel socially adept and confident? Whom do you trust to help you uncover your life's purpose? Write down the names of these people and set up a regular time to discuss your life with each of them.

Mapping Your Direction

Looking back over your freshman-year discoveries, are there any new road maps you need to create? Do you need to check something our by taking a quick detour? What do you need to do to get going in this new direction?

Sophomore Year

Examination

Introduction

Congratulations—you've successfully completed your first year of college! If you've taken the time to start exploring major and career possibilities, you're in a good place right now. The next step is to take stock of what you've learned so far about your passions, innate talents, and what matters most to you. This is a fun stage! You already know the college ropes—now you get to take advantage of all that's available to you.

Examination is the focus of your sophomore year. You'll be critically examining your experiences, potential majors, and, ultimately, career possibilities. As a sophomore, you'll start taking courses in your potential major to gauge whether that major is a good fit for you. You'll meet regularly with academic advisors and career counselors, and begin talking with professors and other students about potential majors. You'll also learn to research internship opportunities as well as companies/organizations you might want to work for in the future. You'll start obtaining impressive experience, too, through leadership opportunities and part-time jobs. You may even decide to take advantage of a study abroad experience. And you'll continue developing your resumé and, eventually, complete at least one *mock interview* (i.e., a practice interview).

Your sophomore year is an exciting time with many potential paths to examine. You'll find that you feel more at home at school, and you'll start figuring out who you are and how that relates to your future. You'll be challenged to learn about yourself through successes as well as the bumps in the road. You'll end up with a deeper understanding of your place in the world and how you can fulfill your life's purpose—at least in part—through your work.

If, at first glance, the tasks and experiences of your sophomore year seem similar to your first-year activities, you're right—to a small degree. But this year, you'll be asked to complete some new activities and take the familiar ones further than before. For example, we asked you during your first year to join a campus organization. This year, we encourage you to consider taking on a minor leadership role in that organization. Through each "year" of this book, you'll build upon the activities of *The College to Career Road Map*—so that by the end of your college years, you'll be ready to pursue the career path that fits you.

Academic Activities

• CONTINUING TASKS •

- Continue using your general education core courses to take a wide variety of classes (see p. 6).

- Continue working with a counselor at your school's career center to pinpoint your interests, skills and abilities, and values (as well as your personality type) (see p. 41).

• NEW TASKS •

Working with a Campus Career Counselor

Explore careers, potential majors, and your unique set of abilities and skills with a campus career counselor.

Why

The vast majority of the careers that exist in the world of work are broader than any one college major. Indeed, in most cases you can choose one of many majors in order to pursue a particular career path. For example: You can major in anything from English or history to biology or engineering and still eventually become an attorney (after law school, of course!).

Some careers do have a specific academic path you must follow. Becoming an actuary, for instance, requires either a math degree or an actuarial science degree. And if you want to become a certified public accountant (CPA), you'll need an accounting degree to prepare yourself for the CPA exam.

All these options! That's why the important task at this time of your college career is to understand the variety of career options that fit you—before you actually settle on a major. You need to look extensively at what's out there.

So do yourself a huge favor: Tap the expertise of the campus professionals around you who want (and who are paid, by you!) to help you choose the best major and career

• TIP •

If you've already chosen your major, you'll still want to continue exploring career possibilities with that major and confirm that your choice is a good fit for you. Every major opens up many doors to various careers— sometimes careers that you didn't even know existed. So work with a career counselor to clarify the reasons why your chosen major and career path make sense for you. You don't want to find out during your senior year that this major really doesn't mesh well with who you are.

path for you! There's absolutely *no* reason for you to tackle this process on your own.

You also don't want to feel pressured to make a choice without really understanding how that choice aligns with your passions, skills and abilities, and values. Do you feel like you were pressured to choose the major you've selected? Then reassess—now—how this decision might impact your life later. Are you willing to live with this choice for at least a few years after you graduate? Do you feel you had enough information to make an informed choice, or do you need to go back and educate yourself more thoroughly?

How

1. Call or stop by your school's career center and set up an appointment to meet with one of the counselors there. Depending on the size of your school, your career center may have anywhere from one counselor to a dozen or more. If you have a choice of counselors to see, try to meet with one who specializes in helping first- and second-year students with choosing a major. (simply ask the person you initially contact at the career center.) Remember: The career center is as interested in connecting you with the right person as *you* are!

2. At your meeting with the career counselor, ask about the key skills and abilities you'll need to succeed in your career areas of interest. Ask about the types of careers you'll be able to pursue with each of the majors you're looking at. Keep your expectations realistic here: Your career counselor isn't going to be able to haul out a list of a hundred specific job titles for every major at your school. But he/she will most certainly be able to teach you how to research these career options on your own. And in many cases, campus career centers do indeed have data on the types of jobs landed by various graduates (with various majors) from their schools. (They gather this information by surveying recent graduates a few months after graduation and compiling the results into a *placement report* that can then be used by other students—like you! So be sure to ask about any placement report[s] that might be available to you.)

3. Ask your career counselor to help you assess each career possibility in terms of other key variables as well—such as your interests and passions, your personality, your values (i.e., what's important to you in a

future career), the future *predicted* job market for people in those careers, and your personal and professional goals.

4. Once you're done brainstorming with your career counselor, go ahead and—as best you can—narrow your list of possible careers down to two or three broad career areas. That's good enough ... for now! Then start looking at the potential majors that would prepare you for these careers. And remember: You can always change your mind later if you want/need to. (And you won't be alone if you do!)

• ROAD MAP QUESTIONS •

Passions: Is there a career field you've always dreamed about? Is there an academic subject/discipline that truly excites you? How does this knowledge tie in to your eventual choices of an academic major and career path?

_____

_____

_____

_____

_____

Innate talents: What are you naturally good at doing? Could you do it for a living? Why or why not? (And if *not* ... are you certain your assessment is accurate? How do you know?)

_____

_____

_____

_____

What matters most: Are there things you do that seem like they're probably a part of your life's purpose? What are they? How could you tie them into your choice of academic major? career?

_____

_____

_____

_____

Meeting with the Academic Advisor

Meet with your academic advisor to explore potential major options that fit with the career areas you're considering.

Why

At most four-year colleges and universities, you'll be required to formally choose your academic major at the end of your sophomore year so that you can register for courses in that major starting junior year. So at some point during your sophomore year, you'll have to switch gears and move from full-fledged major *exploration* to major *decision making*.

The step between these two activities: narrowing down your major choices so that you're seriously considering two to four majors (instead of every major at your school!), from which you'll choose one (or two if you decide to double-major). Make sure the major you choose helps you build the skills and acquire the knowledge necessary to reach success in your chosen career. (Note: Keep in mind that your major doesn't *limit* your career path; rather, it enhances it. It's only one component of your preparation to enter a particular career.)

Your academic advisor will help you understand the requirements of particular careers and majors and how they intersect. Advisors have specific knowledge of your school's major, degree, and institutional requirements. For example, some majors require you to complete a prescribed set of courses before you can apply to the specific program. But for other majors, you can simply declare the major and complete the required coursework before you graduate.

How

1. Early in the first semester of your sophomore year (or sooner if you're so inclined!), contact your academic advisor and set up a meeting with him/her. Tell him/her that you want to use your meeting for the specific purpose of beginning to narrow down your major options. Let him/her know that your goal at this point is to get the number of options down to a manageable level—perhaps somewhere between two and four legitimate possibilities.

2. At your meeting, discuss the careers and majors you've explored so far and which of them interest you the most. Get your advisor's sense of the key skills and abilities you'd need to succeed in each of these careers and majors. Do you have these skills and abilities? Or could you at least develop them?

• T I P •

If you've already declared a major, use this meeting with your academic advisor to make sure you're on track for completing all the requirements for that major.

3. Discuss specific degree requirements with your advisor so that you understand what's required to obtain a degree in a particular major.

• ROAD MAP QUESTIONS •

Passions: Do each of the majors you're considering truly fit *your* interests? Do you really enjoy the subject matter you'll be studying in each of them?

_____

_____

_____

_____

_____

Innate talents: Will you be able to perform well in the classes offered in these majors? How do you know?

_____

_____

_____

_____

What matters most: Will you be studying something that matters to you in these majors, and that will allow you to live the life you want to live (whatever that may entail!) after you graduate?

_____

_____

_____

_____

Choosing a Minor

Explore minors that will complement the majors you're still strongly considering.

Why

You can't major in everything, but if you're like most students you're interested in more than one subject/discipline area. So consider exploring a *minor* area of study to complement the major area of study you ultimately choose (even though most schools don't require a minor for graduation). Not only will a minor diversify your academic experience; it will also give you a more compelling combination of knowledge and skills than you might otherwise gain, making you a better candidate for future internship and job possibilities.

How

1. You've already been exploring potential majors, most of which you will *not* end up pursuing. Talk to your academic advisor and your career counselor to get their ideas on which of these academic disciplines, if any, might make for a good minor for you given the two to four majors you're still considering at this point.

2. Look at the list of minors you're considering. For each of them, consult the department's web site or your undergraduate bulletin to see what courses you'd need to take for each minor and how many credits are involved.

3. Just as you did after exploring majors, come up with a list of two to four *minors* you'd like to seriously think about. That's good enough—for now! Again, you can always change your mind later if you want/need to.

4. Keep in mind that the minor you choose isn't nearly as crucial as the major you choose, at least in the eyes of most employers. You have a bit more flexibility where your minor is concerned—and less pressure to pick the "perfect" discipline. On the scale of life's decisions, the minor you choose is, well, a pretty minor decision!—important, but not a be-all-end-all.

• ROAD MAP QUESTIONS •

Passions: Is there an academic field you like but that you can't or won't pursue as a major?

_____

_____

_____

_____

_____

Innate talents: Is there an academic field (other than your major) that you're good at? Is there a particular skill you can build through a minor that would be valuable in your career areas of interest?

_____

_____

_____

_____

What matters most: Is there an academic field that means enough to you that you'll devote several courses to studying it?

_____

_____

_____

_____

Beginning Major-Course Studies

Sign up for an introductory course or two in the top major you're considering. Take this course no later than the second semester of sophomore year.

Why

You can read a lot about the major you're considering, and you can even talk to students and professors from that major to get their ideas on what the major is all about. But you really won't get a true feel for the major unless and until you take an introductory course or two within that major's academic department. You need to experience the major firsthand—its concepts, its professors, and its students—if you want to have a true sense of how well (or not) it fits *you*.

If you've already declared a major, take these introductory courses in both semesters of your sophomore year. Why? To get a real feel for the major you've chosen. Take the time to reflect upon whether your expectations are in line with what you originally thought this major would offer. If you have a hunch that there are still other majors you'd like to explore, then there's no better time than now to start exploring. You still have plenty of time to change your major to one that truly fits you.

How

1. Unless you covered this task during a previous chat, set up a meeting with your academic advisor shortly before you'll be registering for your courses for the upcoming semester.

2. Ask your advisor to help you choose not only a few courses that count toward your school's core requirements, but also at least one course from the top major you're considering. Select the potential-major course first, then choose and schedule your remaining courses around that one.

3. Choose a backup course in that major department in case you can't get into your first-choice course. Ask your advisor to help you develop a complete backup schedule—built around this backup potential-major course—just in case your first-choice major course falls through. One way or the other, you've *got* to get at least one course from your top potential major into your schedule for the upcoming semester.

• R O A D   M A P   Q U E S T I O N S •

Passions: How do you feel about the potential-major course you've chosen with respect to your interests? Is the course what you thought it would be? Why or why not?

_____

_____

_____

_____

_____

_____

Innate talents: How are you doing in the potential-major course you picked? Do you think you can you handle the work involved in the major you're considering?

_____

_____

_____

_____

_____

What matters most: Does the subject matter of this potential-major course matter to you? Will you be able to apply what you're learning in a real-world career after graduation—so that you can live the life you want to live (whatever that may entail!)?

_____

_____

_____

_____

_____

Evaluating Academic Progress

Meet with your academic advisor to critically evaluate your academic progress.

Why

You pretty much *have* to meet with your academic advisor at least once a semester, if only to get him/her to sign off on your proposed schedule of courses for the next semester. If you stop there, however, you won't really get to know your advisor very well—nor will he/she get to know you. Moreover, you won't be able to tap his/her knowledge of your school's academic programs and corresponding post-graduation career opportunities.

If, on the other hand, you set up a second meeting to review your academic progress—perhaps around mid-semester or shortly thereafter, (a) you'll stand out in your advisor's

If you've already declared a major, meeting with your academic advisor is key to staying on task and assessing how you're doing academically. That way, nothing will slip through the cracks and you'll be ready to graduate on time.

mind as a student who takes his/her college experience seriously, and (b) you'll become one of the few advisees your advisor actually proactively collaborates with—and not just a vaguely familiar face who shows up once a semester to have his/her course schedule approved during a two-minute, largely artificial interaction.

How

1. Set up a meeting with your academic advisor a week or two after your midterm exams are done. Ask your advisor to help you review your academic progress so far, including how you're moving toward your degree and graduation requirements.

2. Look at your cumulative grade point average (GPA) so far. If you're struggling, ask your advisor to give you the name of a key person or office on campus that can help you raise your grades. Does your school have a Learning Center (or similarly named office), for example, or an office where you can work with a tutor for the course that's driving you nuts?

3. Step away from your grades for a minute and ask your advisor to help you identify which courses you've *enjoyed* the most so far (and why), as well as which ones you've enjoyed the least (and why). Ask your advisor if he/she can help you pinpoint key likes and dislikes that have emerged from your coursework to date.

• ROAD MAP QUESTIONS •

Passions: Do you find that you always study for a particular course first? last? Why do you think you operate this way?

_____

_____

_____

_____

_____

Innate talents: Are you more successful in a particular course? What skills and abilities do you possess that make it easier to do well in this course?

_____

_____

_____

_____

What matters most: Do any of your courses fit with your heart? Do any of them seem especially meaningful to you? Why?

_____

_____

_____

_____

Preparing for Studying Abroad

Firm up any plans you have for studying abroad later in your sophomore year, during a J-term (January term), during your junior year, or during an upcoming summer.

Why

Studying abroad is one of the best ways to gain exposure to the world around you and learn about a culture that's different from your own—both experiences that employers value highly in new college graduates (see pps. 22-23 of Freshman Year), especially in our increasingly global world economy and job market. If an employer knows you can work well with people (e.g., clients, colleagues) from another culture—and perhaps even live *within* that culture without any major problems—he/she is much more likely to hire *you* vs. another recent grad who doesn't have this background.

How

1. If you haven't already done so, ask your academic advisor or a counselor at your school's career center if your institution has a Study Abroad office or department. (Alternatively, look for mentions of one on your school's web site.)

2. Call, email, or stop by the Study Abroad office and ask for general information on study abroad opportunities offered through your school. (You'll generally receive a brochure and some application materials, or perhaps the address of a web site to visit.)

3. Ask if you can meet individually with an advisor in the study abroad office, or if there are any upcoming introductory sessions for students like you who are interested in potentially studying abroad. If you can do either, or both, of these things, do so!

4. Ask your academic advisor, your professors, your campus career counselor, and your friends if they know anyone who is currently studying abroad or who has done so in the past. Get the names and contact information of these students/grads. Then contact them—in person or via phone or email—and ask them what studying abroad is really like. (Who better to tell you than students/grads from your school who have studied abroad themselves?)

5. Check out the web sites of organizations like the Council on International Educational Exchange (www.ciee.org) and the Institute of International Education (www.iie.org) to learn more about study abroad possibilities.

6. Decide which study abroad experience you want to pursue and complete the appropriate paperwork for it. Send in your application, with applicable fees, long before the application deadline to ensure you'll be considered.

7. Once you know where you'll be studying abroad, work closely with your academic advisor and/or the school's study abroad coordinator to make key preparations ahead of time—e.g., where you'll live in your host country, what you'll study and where, places where you can look for a job there (if applicable to your situation), and people you can contact for help once you're in the country.

8. During your study abroad experience, keep a detailed journal or diary of your daily activities. What new skills are you learning? What surprises or excites you about this new culture? What are you struggling with? Keep track of it all—not only for your own trip down memory lane years from now, but also for resumé development and interviewing purposes once you're back home!

• ROAD MAP QUESTIONS •

Passions: Do you enjoy new adventures, exploring the unknown, and learning about a culture that's different—perhaps very different—from your own? Why or why not? What is it about the idea of studying abroad that appeals to you?

_____

_____

_____

_____

_____

_____

Innate talents: Are you able to roll with change and survive—even thrive—in a strange environment? If you study in a non-English-speaking country, do you have the foreign language skills necessary to function there on a day-to-day basis? Are you naturally adaptable, flexible, and open-minded? How well do you do when you don't know, ahead of time, what problems and issues you're going to have to deal with?

_____

_____

_____

_____

_____

_____

What matters most: Do you believe it's valuable, in and of itself, to understand cultures that are different from your own and, from a career perspective, to pursue a career that at least occasionally takes you outside the country? Will your time studying abroad give you experiences that are important to you and your future career aspirations?

_____

_____

_____

_____

_____

_____

_____

_____

Getting to Know Your Professors

Expand your efforts to get to know your professors; go beyond knowing just *one* of them.

Why

The diversity among the professors at your school—particularly in terms of their knowledge bases and areas of expertise—is amazing. If you're in career and major exploration mode (which you are at this point), doesn't it make sense to talk to as many of your instructors as possible to learn more about their academic departments (and the potential careers you could pursue by majoring in their disciplines)? Why *wouldn't* you want to be introduced to as many different ideas as possible?

How

1. What's your favorite course this semester? Next time you have this class, take a moment immediately after the class session to talk to the

professor before he/she leaves the room. Tell him/her that you're finding the course topics genuinely interesting and that you're in the process of exploring what to major in.

Getting to know your professors is an essential task whether you've declared a major or not. Professors can lend a helpful ear and give great advice. They also have real-world contacts—oftentimes alumni/ae of your school— who may be helpful to you in some way. Getting to know a variety of professors is a fabulous way to expand your knowledge about the career possibilities your chosen major offers— or even those of another major you haven't yet considered.

2. Ask the professor if he/she would be willing to meet with you sometime soon to discuss not the course per se, but what it's like to major in that course's discipline. If he/she *is* willing to meet, see if you can get on his/her schedule right then and there.

3. Go to your scheduled meeting prepared to take the lead in your discussion with the professor. When he/she invariably asks, "So … what is it that you wanted to talk about?", you need to be ready to say something like this: "I'm thinking about what to major in right now, and _____ is on my list of possibilities. Could you tell me a little bit about this major? What kinds of jobs do people use this major for? What skills will I learn?"

4. Take a few notes on the professor's suggestions and ask him/her if there are *other* things you can do to explore the major (e.g., talking to other professors in the department, reading books, visiting web sites).

5. Repeat this same process with the instructors you have for *other* courses you find interesting. All you have to do is show genuine interest in their disciplines; invariably, your talks with them will help them remember you not as "just another student in one of my classes," but as one of those rare students who seems to truly care about what he/she is learning and why.

• ROAD MAP QUESTIONS •

Passions: Are there any professors you're drawn to and excited to be around because they hold your interest? What's so appealing about them?

_____

_____

_____

_____

Innate talents: Is there anything you're consistently complimented on by your professors? Do they point out to you what might not be obvious to you—that you're good at a certain something? How come you've never recognized this key skill or ability yourself? Could the same be true of other skills and abilities you have?

_____

_____

_____

_____

What matters most: Are you finding that your values mesh well with what you're experiencing as you talk to different professors? Why or why not?

_____

_____

_____

_____

Talking to Upperclassmen

Talk to upperclassmen in the majors you're considering; see what *they* have to say about their chosen disciplines.

Why

It's great whenever you can read about a particular major in a book or on a web site, but you'll get another essential perspective by talking to the *students* who are in that major right now. Not only will they know which courses are interesting (or not) and which professors fit your learning style (or not); they'll also be aware of internships their fellow students (or they themselves) are doing within the major, and perhaps even the entry-level jobs landed by their slightly older peers who have graduated from the major in the last year or two.

In short, upperclassmen in the majors you're considering will be among your best sources of learning about the day-to-day realities of being in that major, as well as the future internship and job possibilities within that major.

If you've already declared a major, talking to upperclassmen is a great way to connect with students who have already successfully maneuvered through much of the major you're in. They may have some very helpful advice on professors' teaching styles that could help you choose your class schedule more wisely. They also may know something about the major that you don't, which may impact your thoughts about that major. Moreover, they can give you a clearer idea of what you need to do to be successful in the major, both in and out of class.

How

1. If it's clear that there are a few upperclassmen in one of your courses in a discipline of interest, catch one of them before or after class and ask if he/she would be willing to tell you a bit more about the major from

his/her perspective. What's good about it? What's bad? What internships and jobs has he/she heard of other students/grads landing with that major?

2. Go to your school's Student Organizations or Student Activities (or similarly named) office and ask if there are any student groups related to the major that are of strong interest to you. For example, if you're taking an introductory public relations course and you find yourself getting a kick out of it, ask if your school has a related campus organization like the Public Relations Student Society of America (www.prssa.org). If it does, contact one of the leaders of the group (the Student Organizations or Student Activities office will have a listing of each group's leadership) or visit its web site to see when the group meets on campus. Mark your calendar to attend the group's next meeting as a prospective member who wants to learn more about the organization. Most groups will welcome you with open arms—and their upperclass student leaders will be glad to answer your questions about the discipline.

3. If you live in a residence hall or apartment where juniors and seniors also live, ask one or more of them if they happen to be majoring in the discipline you're interested in (or if they know of *other* upperclassmen who are majoring in that discipline). Ask these students if they'd be willing to tell you about the major and what they've learned about it so far.

• ROAD MAP QUESTIONS •

Passions: Does the major you're learning about seem to focus on topics and challenges you really enjoy? Will you like going to your classes, or dread it?

_____

_____

_____

_____

Innate talents: Will you be able to perform well in the courses within this major, academically speaking, based on what you're hearing from the upperclass students?

_____

_____

_____

_____

What matters most: Do the students you've talked to seem passionate about what they're studying? Is it clear that what they're studying matters to them and has application in a real-world career after graduation?

_____

_____

_____

_____

Focusing on the Professors in Your Potential Majors

Talk to professors in the majors you're considering; see what they have to say about their chosen disciplines.

Why

It's one thing to get the student perspective on a major that interests you. But unlike your fellow undergraduates, the *professors* in the majors that interest you have obviously demonstrated a significant commitment to it by studying it for years and, in most cases, earning a doctoral degree in it so that they can teach it and research it at the college level. Clearly, then, they must feel very strongly about that discipline. You can easily find out why—and whether you, too, might share this passion and turn it into some sort of career someday. But you need to *ask*. Professors won't come to you on the off chance you might be interested in what they have to say; you have to show them you're interested.

Usually, once you demonstrate genuine interest in it, a professor will talk your ear off about his/her discipline. After all … it's the topic he/she has committed to for the long haul.

If you've already chosen your major, seek out professors in that major so you can develop good networking contacts for potential internships or even jobs later. Who knows—one of these professors might even become a professional reference for you someday! It's always good to have a professor know you as a person—as someone beyond just a student in his/her class—because he/she can then speak more specifically to prospective employers (or graduate/ professional school programs) about your skills, knowledge, and interests. The more specific your professors can be when they talk about you, the better their references will be and the more weight those references will carry.

How

1. Once you have a major/discipline in mind that you'd like to learn more about, go to your school's web site and find the link to the web site of that major's/discipline's academic department at your school. (Generally you'll find this information under a broad heading like "Academics" or "Programs and Majors.")

2. Once you're on the major's/discipline's web site, look for a link called "Faculty" (or something similar)—basically, the place on the site that lists the names and contact information of all faculty members within the department.

3. Look for a professor or two who seems like he/she might be a good person for you to talk to according to his/her biographical information and/or position. Is there a professor, for example, who advises an on-campus organization for students in that major department? Is there a professor who has published papers or spoken at conferences on a topic that really grabs you? Is there a professor who, fairly or unfairly, has a photograph that makes him/her look friendly and approachable? (Or, alternatively, is there a professor you've heard about through the student grapevine as being friendly and enthusiastic toward students? Note: If you haven't tapped the student grapevine already, now's the time!)

4. Decide how you'd like to approach this professor about discussing his/her discipline. Depending on your personality, you may be most comfortable simply stopping by the professor's office out of the blue to ask for a meeting ... or calling him/her to ask for a meeting ... or emailing him/her to ask for a meeting. *How* you ask for a meeting with the professor doesn't matter; *that* you ask is what counts.

5. Tell the professor you're exploring the possibility of majoring in his/her discipline, but that you'd like to learn more about it before you make your final decision. Ask him/her if he/she would be willing to talk with you for, say, twenty minutes so you could ask a few basic questions.

6. The vast majority of professors will gladly talk to you about their disciplines—if you ask. A few, however, will say "no" to you (for various reasons). Don't be alarmed by this development—and, much more importantly, don't conclude that *all* of the professors in the department will treat you this way ... because they won't. Instead, just find another

professor to approach with your request. Keep asking around until you find a professor who's willing to chat with you.

7. During your chat with the professor, ask him/her what's good about his/her discipline. What's bad about it? And what internships and jobs has he/she heard of students/graduates landing with that particular major?

8. Wrap up your meeting by asking the professor about other things you can do to learn more about the major/discipline. Are there other people you can talk to? books you can read? web sites you can visit?

• ROAD MAP QUESTIONS •

Passions: Do the professors you've talked to exude a joy for what they do? Is their discipline something that speaks to you, too? Why or why not?

_____

_____

_____

_____

Innate talents: Will you be able to hold your own in this major's courses, academically speaking, based on what you've heard from the professors you've talked to?

_____

_____

_____

_____

What matters most: Do the professors you've talked to seem passionate about what they're studying/teaching? Is it clear that what they're studying/teaching matters and has applications in the world of work after graduation?

_____

_____

_____

_____

Experiential Activities

• CONTINUING TASKS •

- Continue looking for ways to volunteer (see p. 32 of Freshman Year).
- Continue collecting items for your career portfolio (see p. 37 of Freshman Year).

• NEW TASKS •

Pursuing a Leadership Role in a Campus Organization

Pursue a leadership role in at least one campus organization on campus.

Why

It's one thing to participate in a campus organization. But employers who hire new college graduates consistently report that they're looking for grads who have _leadership_ skills and experience. (Not convinced? Review the results of the "soft skills" survey of employers on p. 29 of Freshman Year.)

Leading a student group is a natural way for you to develop sound leadership skills—not to mention many other skills that will help you in your future career (e.g., team building, organization, conceptualizing ideas).

How

1. If you're already a member of a campus organization, ask one of its current leaders about leadership opportunities *you* can pursue within the group. Pick one of those opportunities and go for it!

2. If you're not currently in a campus organization, go to your school's Student Activities or Student Organizations (or similarly named) office to see which groups exist at your school. Pick one or two that sound interesting and see if they have web sites or information blurbs in your undergraduate bulletin or student handbook. Usually, the number of choices is amazing—you can participate in everything from the biology club to the water ski club! Then, contact leaders or members of these groups to see what leadership opportunities exist, particularly at lower levels (since you're new to each of these groups, after all). If a lower-level leadership position is available and open to you in an organization of interest, apply for it.

3. If you aren't able to land a leadership role in a campus organization at this time, talk to the leaders of the organizations that interest you and get their advice on how you can best prepare to land a leadership position during your *junior* year.

• ROAD MAP QUESTIONS •

Passions: Do you like the idea of being a leader? Why or why not? Do you enjoy influencing your peers? Why or why not?

_____

_____

_____

_____

_____

Innate talents: Are you good at being a leader? Do people naturally follow you? Do you have good interpersonal skills? How do you know?

_____

_____

_____

_____

_____

_____

_____

_____

What matters most: Do you have compassion for others? Do you enjoy improving organizations and systems for the greater good? Why or why not?

_____

_____

_____

_____

_____

_____

_____

_____

Campus Leadership Positions

Explore applying for one of the unique campus leadership positions at your school.

Why

Who are the student leaders you've seen at your school—Resident Assistants, Community Advisors, Admissions Ambassadors, Orientation Leaders, Alumni Ambassadors, Peer Advisors, Health Advocates, and others? They stand out on campus, don't they? They stand out to future employers, too.

Typically these positions require a tremendous amount of responsibility. The students in these roles have been selected and trained. They're also well embedded within in the campus community—a situation that affords them many opportunities that other students simply don't get.

These unique campus leadership roles also help you build sound communication, problem-solving, and critical thinking skills—not to mention a a solid professional reference from at least one mid-level or even high-level campus administrator.

How

1. Typically, the campus offices/departments that offer these types of unique leadership positions are: Residence Life (Housing Services), First-Year Programs, Orientation, Admissions, Health Services, and Alumni Relations. Contact these offices (or visit their web sites) to find out about the opportunities that are available, the selection processes for them, and the minimum requirements to apply.

2. If your campus has a separate Leadership Office, ask someone there about the variety of opportunities on your campus to get involved and build some leadership skills. Chances are, there are leadership possibilities you aren't even aware of—yet!

3. Usually these unique campus leadership positions are highly sought after and have a fairly competitive selection process. (That's why the students who land them are so desirable to graduate/professional programs and prospective employers alike.) The process often involves several interviews (individual or group), a written application complete with essay questions, and a written reference from someone who can discuss your people skills, dependability, organizational skills, communication skills, and problem-solving skills.

• ROAD MAP QUESTIONS •

Passions: Do you enjoy leading your peers in broad-based activities? Do you have an interest in taking on significant responsibilities? Why or why not?

_____

_____

_____

_____

Innate talents: Do you have solid communication skills, problem-solving skills, and critical thinking skills—or could you develop them? Are you self-directed?

_____

_____

_____

_____

What matters most: Do you enjoy helping others learn and develop? What value do you see in being able to influence your peers?

_____

_____

_____

_____

Is Your Part-Time Job Providing Learning Opportunities?

Assess your part-time job to ensure it's providing sound learning opportunities for you. (And if it isn't, consider finding a different part-time job.)

Why

Almost 75 percent of full-time college students work while attending school to help pay for their college expenses, according to the U.S. Department of Education. And of the students who do work, the Department of Education says, 71 percent do so for fifteen hours a week or more.

Up until this time in your college career, working—in and of itself—was probably enough to be of benefit to you where your long-term career interests are concerned. But now you need to evaluate whether or not you're being challenged in your job and if it is helping you move toward the career of your choice. A part-time job can (and should) be more than just a paycheck; it can help you build the key skills and traits that will be sought by future employers, give you valuable experience, and help you make important contacts in the world of work.

How

1. Make a list of the skills and traits you're building in your current part-time job. (If you don't have a part-time job right now, make a list of the skills you've developed in previous jobs.) Are these skills *transferable* skills—that is, key skills (e.g., communication, teamwork, self-motivation) you'll need to be successful in *any* career you might pursue? If so, continue working to build these skills. And if not, consider looking for another part-time job—one that will teach you these skills.

2. If you find that you do indeed need to look for a different part-time job, write down some general ideas about the type of job you'd like to get. What activities should it encompass? What would you like to try? What opportunities would challenge you to learn something new? Write these criteria down so that you have a crystal clear list of what your next part-time job needs to "look" like.

3. Review the ideas from Freshman Year (see p. 34) on finding a part-time job so that you can track down a wide variety of opportunities using a wide variety of resources.

4. Consider the following practical questions:

- How much do you need to be paid to earn the amount of money you need for school?
- Where (location) must you work so you can actually get to your job each day?
- Are you limited in any way in the type of job you can pursue? How so?

• ROAD MAP QUESTIONS •

Passions: Is there something you're doing (or could do) in your part-time job that would align well with your natural passions? If not, is there anything you could do to change the situation, even if only slightly?

_____

_____

_____

_____

_____

Innate talents: What are the essential skills you need to learn through your part-time job that are critical to your future career success?

_____

_____

_____

_____

_____

What matters most: Is there a company/organization you could work for that fits your most cherished values? If so, have you checked to see about part-time job openings there?

_____

_____

_____

_____

_____

Revising Your Resumé

Revise your resumé to reflect the experiences, skills, and accomplishments you gained during freshman year and the summer following freshman year.

Why

A resumé is a living document that needs to change as you change and grow. It would be foolish for you to write your resumé once and then rest on it. After all, as you progress through your college years, you gain more and more experiences, skills, and accomplishments to brag about!

How

1. Make an appointment with a counselor at your school's career center and let him/her know you'd like to spend your time together revising your resumé.

2. Before your appointment, take three sheets of paper and label them "New Experiences," "New Skills," and "New Accomplishments," respectively.

3. Take your "New Experiences" sheet and start jotting down any new experiences you can think of that have occurred between your freshman year and now. _Do not limit yourself at this point!_ If something jumps into your mind—no matter how minor or insignificant it might seem—

write it down! The idea is to do a "brain dump" and get everything out of your head and onto paper. Later, you and your career counselor can decide what to add to your resumé and what to leave off.

4. Go through the same "brain dump" exercise with your "New Skills" and "New Accomplishments" sheets. Again, *do not limit yourself at this point!*

5. Once you've finished writing down everything you can think of on each of the sheets, keep them in a handy spot ... just in case you think of other entries to add later.

6. Bring the sheets to your appointment with the career counselor and tell him/her you've written down everything you can think of. Ask him/her to help you remember anything you may have forgotten or disregarded.

7. With the counselor's help, decide which entries to add to your resumé and which to leave off. You'll almost certainly have to do some reformatting of your resumé to accommodate the changes—don't be alarmed by that.

8. Once you've finished revising your resumé, set up another appointment and ask your career counselor to look at your resumé one last time (for now, at least!) for minor revisions.

• ROAD MAP QUESTIONS •

Passions: Does your resumé effectively reflect what you're passionate about? How do you know?

_____

_____

_____

_____

_____

Innate talents: Are your innate talents and skills effectively highlighted on your resumé? How can you be sure?

_____

_____

_____

What matters most: Does your resumé speak clearly about what you represent and what matters to you?

_____

_____

_____

Utilizing Informational Interviews

Conduct *informational interviews* to research careers in more depth by not only reading about them, but also talking (in person or via phone/email) to people who actually work in them.

Why

It's one thing to read about a particular career in a book or on a web site. But it's quite another to talk to people who actually work in that career. That's what *informational interviewing* is all about.

The people who work in a particular career of interest will be able to tell you about subtleties and nuances that books and web sites can't possibly cover. They'll also be able to describe how their specific organizations work, how they themselves chose their fields, and what they had to do to land a job.

How

1. Choose a field/industry or company/organization you'd like to learn more about—in depth.

2. Ask people you already know—relatives, professors, friends, your academic advisor, your career counselor—if they have any contacts in the field/industry or company/organization you'd like to research.

3. If one of the people you already know *does* know someone you could talk to, ask him/her to first contact that person on your behalf ... to feel out whether it would be OK for *you* to contact the person directly. (Note: It almost always *is* OK!) This tactic will help you significantly because it will prepare the person for your initial contact later; that way you won't be contacting him/her out of the blue, as a *complete* stranger.

4. If the people you already know *do not* know someone you could talk to, make an appointment with a counselor at your school's career center. Let him/her know in advance that the purpose of your meeting is for you to find one or more informational interviewing contacts in the field/industry or company/organization you want to learn more about. It may take a bit of time and investigation, but together your career counselor and you will be able to find at least one potential contact (and probably far more than one!).

5. Once you've identified a person you want to get in touch with, decide *how* to approach that person in a way that best fits your personality. If you're more outgoing and extraverted, for example, you might be most comfortable giving the person a call. But if you're more reserved and introverted, you might feel better writing to or emailing the person instead. *Use whatever approach works best for you!*

6. In your approach call/email/letter, tell the person who you are, where you're going to school, and what you're trying to learn (e.g., "I'm trying to find out more about the _____ field"). Reassure the person that you're *not* interested in hitting him/her up for a job. Rather, you're simply looking for information and advice.

7. Ask the person if he/she would be willing to meet with you for thirty minutes sometime soon so you could ask him/her a few basic questions about his/her field/industry and/or company/organization.

8. The vast majority (80 percent or better) of the time, the person will be glad to meet with you. If that's the case this time, go ahead and set up an appointment. (Note: If the person is unwilling or unable to meet with you, politely thank him/her for his/her time and approach another person instead.)

9. Before your meeting, write down the basic questions you'd like to ask the person. You can use common sense to come up with most of your

questions (e.g., "What do you do in your job?"), but you can get additional ideas from a career counselor (or a book) at your school's career center.

10. Dress nicely for your informational interview, show up on time, and greet your informational interviewee with a warm "Hello" and introductory handshake. If it so happens that you'll be meeting the person at a coffee shop, restaurant, etc., be sure to *insist* on buying!

11. Write down a few notes during your meeting and keep track of any new questions that pop into your head.

12. Stick firmly to the thirty minutes you asked for. Be prepared to close the meeting once those thirty minutes have elapsed. However, if the person insists that it's OK for the two of you to talk a little longer, go ahead and do so.

13. Once the meeting is over, shake the person's hand again, thank him/her profusely, and then go home and *immediately* write a thank-you note to him/her. Be sure it's in the mail within twenty-four hours of your meeting.

• ROAD MAP QUESTIONS •

Passions: After talking with someone in a career that interests you, has your interest in the career grown? decreased? Does what you learned about the career match up with what you've learned by reading about that career?

_____

_____

_____

_____

Innate talents: Do you believe you'll be able to perform successfully in that career? Why or why not? Are you more confident in your ability to handle the job? less confident? Why?

_____

_____

_____

_____

_____

_____

_____

_____

What matters most: Will you be able to do and achieve most of the things that are important to you by pursuing this particular career? How do you know? How did your informational interviewee help you affirm (or disaffirm) this conclusion?

_____

_____

_____

_____

_____

_____

_____

_____

Creating an "Internship/Co-op Possibilities" Binder

Create an "Internship/Co-op Possibilities" binder by researching internship and co-op possibilities. (Or, if you can, go ahead and actually *do* an internship or a co-op!)

Why

At some point during your college career (the sooner the better!), you should complete at least one internship or a co-op experience. Why? Well, a few schools (to their great credit) require it. But there's a much more important reason too: Today's employers expect you to come out of college with at least *some* hands-on experience in your chosen field. If you don't, you'll have difficulty competing against a substantial number of your peers—who *will* have internship and/or co-op experience.

If you choose not to bother with an internship or a co-op, you'll be competing for an entry-level job with students and recent grads who *have* done internships and/or co-ops (often more than one!). And that contest won't last long—for you'll be unable to compete, given your relative lack of experience.

There are many internship and co-op opportunities available to you. But you probably won't pursue any of them until *next* year (i.e., your junior year). That's why it's so

• FACT •

In the 2005 Graduating Student & Alumni Survey *conducted by the National Association of Colleges and Employers (a trade association for college/university career services professionals and employers who hire new college graduates), 39.4 percent of the 750+ students surveyed said they'd completed at least one internship during college, and 8.1 percent said they'd completed at least one co-op experience.*

In the 2005 College Graduation Survey *conducted by Monster-TRAK (the college student/recent graduate web site of online job site Monster), 59 percent of the nearly 11,000 college students surveyed said they'd completed at least one internship during college.*

In the 2005 College Graduate Career Survey *conducted by Experience (a career web site for college students/recent graduates), 67 percent of the 6,500 students surveyed said they'd completed at least one internship.*

important for you to start keeping track of internships and/or co-ops you learn about *this* year (i.e., your sophomore year). By simply printing out information about them and keeping the materials in your possession, you'll be able to effectively do just that—so that next year (or sooner) you'll have some solid leads on internships or co-ops you can try to *land*.

How

1. Here are several specific ways you can begin uncovering future internship and co-op possibilities:

    • Visit your school's career center (or its web site) and read the internship and co-op listings it has obtained from specific organizations.

    • Check out a college-oriented career web site like MonsterTRAK (www.monstertrak.com), Experience (www.experience.com), CollegeGrad (www.collegegrad.com), or CollegeRecruiter (www.collegerecruiter.com) and look for internship and co-op listings there.

    • Go to your campus library or a nearby bookstore and look through one of the many printed internship directories that are on the market (published annually by companies like Princeton Review and Peterson's). (Note: At the bookstore, you'll find such guides in the "Careers" or "College Guides" section.)

    • Talk to professors and fellow students and ask them where current and previous students from your school/department have done internships or co-ops in the past. (Note: Employers often prefer hiring new interns/co-op students from the same schools/departments where they've had success doing so in the past. Take advantage of this phenomenon!)

    • Talk to a counselor at your school's career center (particularly if your school's center has an *internship coordinator* or similarly titled person on staff). Ask him/her where previous students from your school have interned or done co-ops in the past.

    • Directly approach organizations that interest you and ask (by phone or email) whether they have internship or co-op opportunities for college students. If they do, ask how you can learn more about those possibilities.

2. As you come across internship and co-op possibilities that interest you, write down key details about them in a notebook or, better yet, photocopy or print the information you find and keep it all in a three-ring binder labeled "Internship/Co-op Possibilities." You'll be coming back to this critical information just a few months from now (or sooner)—so make sure it's well organized and easy for you to find.

• ROAD MAP QUESTIONS •

Passions: What career or field are you drawn to explore in depth—and in a very practical, hands-on kind of way—by working in it for a few months via an internship or a co-op? Why?

_____

_____

_____

Innate talents: What career or field might be one in which you'll excel—or in which you may excel if given the opportunity to try it via an internship or a co-op? Why?

_____

_____

_____

What matters most: What career or field might be one in which you do work that aligns well with your values (i.e., what's important to you)? Why?

_____

_____

_____

Developing a "Dream Companies" Binder

Develop a "Dream Companies" binder by researching companies/organizations you think you *might* want to work for someday.

Why

At some point during the upcoming months, you'll need to narrow your choices down to a few companies/organizations you want to focus on for your internship, co-op, and, eventually, job search activities. (You can't work everywhere after all!) So this is the time to begin doing some initial research on companies/organizations that interest you.

At this point, you don't have to know everything there is to know about various companies/organizations; but it is important for you to know *something* about the places you may want to approach later to seek an internship, a co-op, or an entry-level job. By organizing this type of information from the start—and hanging onto it in a safe place—you'll be able to draw upon it throughout the rest of your college career and, especially, during your future job searches.

How

1. Visit the web sites of companies/organizations that interest you and have a look around. What do these companies/organizations do, generally speaking? What do their values seem to be? Is there any evidence that they have big plans for future expansion or growth? And do they appear to offer internship, co-op, or entry-level job opportunities?

2. Start reading a daily newspaper (in print or online) so you can keep an eye out for mentions of your target companies/organizations. What are various media outlets writing about "your" companies/organizations?

3. Go to your campus library and ask a reference librarian there to show you how to use online databases like Lexis/Nexis and ProQuest to search for articles about "your" companies/organizations in trade publications and other off-the-beaten-path media outlets. What are these publications writing about "your" companies/organizations?

4. Ask your professors, friends, parents, academic advisor, career counselor, and anyone else you can think of if they know anything about "your" target companies/organizations. For example, does one of the

counselors at your school's career center regularly interact with a recruiter from one of "your" companies/organizations? If so, what has the counselor learned about the company/organization through his/her interactions with the recruiter?

5. As you find information about particular companies/organizations that resonate with you, keep it in a "Dream Companies" binder. Make photocopies of the information or print it out, and organize it by company. You'll be able to use this information later in your college career—when you begin interviewing for an internship, a co-op, or a job.

• ROAD MAP QUESTIONS •

Passions: Which companies/organizations are doing or making things that really grab your attention in a positive way? What, specifically, is so intriguing about these organizations?

_____

_____

_____

_____

_____

_____

_____

_____

_____

_____

_____

Innate talents: As you research companies/organizations, what patterns or trends do you see in terms of the skills/abilities required for working in those companies/organizations? What *hard* skills (e.g., writing, balancing a ledger) and *soft* skills (e.g., working well with other people, taking initiative) are most frequently mentioned as being critical to success?

_____

_____

_____

_____

_____

_____

_____

What matters most: Which companies/organizations seem to value the things you value (or most of them, at least)? And which companies/organizations offer career opportunities that will allow you to live the life you want to live after graduation (whatever that may entail)?

_____

_____

_____

_____

_____

_____

_____

_____

Mock Interviews

Do a few *mock interviews* (i.e., practice interviews) with a campus career counselor (or someone else) so that you can polish your interviewing skills.

Why

Interviewing, for most college students, is a weird and stressful experience—especially the first few times! Where else do you feel such pressure to be "on" and to perform well in front of a bunch of strangers?

It's critical for you to practice interviewing—in a setting where it's OK to make mistakes and then improve upon them. That's what *mock interviewing* is all about. Sadly, too few college students take advantage of mock interviewing—only to watch as their more-interview-savvy peers land the best internships, co-ops, and jobs. Don't let this happen to you!

How

1. Contact your school's career center and set up an appointment with one of the counselors there. (Note: It's best if you can briefly talk to the counselor you'll be meeting with. Tell him/her that you'd like to do a mock interview, and give him/her some details about the type of internship/job you'd like to "interview" for, and with what "organization.")

2. A few days before your mock interview, email your resumé to the counselor you'll be working with so that he/she can effectively prepare for the discussion ahead of time. At the same time, ask the counselor if it's possible for him/her to videotape (or at least audiotape) your mock interview. If it is, tell the counselor you'd like to go ahead and do that. (This will allow him/her to set up the appropriate equipment ahead of time.)

3. Prepare for the mock interview as best you can, knowing it won't go perfectly (not even close!). Remember: The idea at this point is not to do everything right, but to *learn* how to do everything right.

4. On the day of your mock interview, dress just as you would for the real thing. (That way the counselor can evaluate not only your interview performance but your attire and "look" as well.)

5. When you arrive at the career center for your mock interview, you'll most likely go right into "interview" mode (just as you would for the

real thing). So be prepared for the counselor to start playing his/her "employer" role right off the bat ... the moment you walk in the door. Remember: The idea is to simulate, as realistically as possible, the feel of an actual interview—complete with those somewhat awkward first few moments.

6. During the time you're being "interviewed," stay in your role as the job/internship seeker. Don't slip in any asides to the counselor that you wouldn't say to an actual employer. You want to be sure that your mock interview is as realistic as possible—and that includes you being a little nervous!

7. Once your mock interview is done, debrief with your counselor immediately. (If you recorded the interview, watch or listen to it immediately.) Start by telling the counselor what *you* think you did well and not so well. Then ask the counselor what you did well and not so well.

8. Write down the things you did well and, especially, the things you and your counselor feel you need to work on. You can practice these activities in additional mock interviews (a great idea!) or even, more informally, with family members and friends who are willing to ask questions of you.

9. Be prepared to do more than one mock interview. (Most everyone needs at least two.) Much like riding a bike, interviewing gets easier with sheer practice. And that practice requires time and energy on your part. There are no shortcuts.

• ROAD MAP QUESTIONS •

Passions: Does your passion for your chosen career (or the company/organization you're "interviewing" with) come across in your responses during the mock interview? How do you know?

_____

_____

_____

_____

Innate talents: Does interviewing come pretty easily and naturally to you, or is it a skill you'll have to work on? Do you need to practice telling people about your strengths and key accomplishments? Will you do yourself justice in your interviews for internships and/or jobs? How can you say for sure?

_____

_____

_____

What matters most: Do you know how to share your values appropriately? Are you able to explain why you'd be a good fit with a particular organization and _its_ values?

_____

_____

_____

_____

dreams ... discoveries ... reflections ...
intentions ... discussions

➤—◆—➤

Mapping Your Direction

Uncovering Your Purpose
Sophomore Year

"The true profession of man is to find his way to himself."
~ HERMANN HESSE

Now that you're in your sophomore year, your focus will be on examining your experiences and courses so far—and determining how you feel about what you're doing so that you can make some key decisions by the end of this year (such as what major to declare, for example, or whether or not you'd like to study abroad or pursue an internship).

This year, it's important for you to truly connect to who you are and who you want to become. Why? Because it's the best way for you to choose a meaningful, well-fitting academic major and, ultimately, a satisfying post-college career. It's time to find your own path—a winding one, no doubt (if you're like most people, at least!), but one you'll continue on for the rest of your life.

You'll do this important work by exploring, examining, experiencing, and questioning everything that's important to you. You need to awaken that portion of yourself that is often hidden—sometimes by fear, sometimes by the many other voices in your life telling you to do something else. Quiet those outside voices and listen to the most important one—the one within you. This is the voice that will lead you to finding your true purpose.

Purpose

Are you living life your way? How so? What urges do you have that might be connected to your purpose? Have you started to connect to the things that hold meaning and purpose for you?

_____

_____

_____

_____

_____

_____

_____

_____

_____

_____

_____

_____

Dreams—Life's Destinations

Do you have a deep inner desire to make sense of your life and the world around you? What are the opportunities you've experienced that have impacted you this past year? When have you felt totally fulfilled or inspired by something new—something that might become a part of your life dreams?

Discoveries

Scenic highways: How have you felt connected with your purpose this year? What has life been whispering to you? What do you feel deeply about or ponder every now and then that is truly important to you? (Examples: Perhaps you're thinking of living somewhere completely different—or becoming a specialist in a unique area of research because the learning itself moves you.)

_____

_____

_____

_____

_____

_____

Roadblocks and speed bumps: What opportunities have you turned down because of fear or uncertainty? What do you want to do about it?

_____

_____

_____

_____

_____

_____

_____

_____

Reflections

Have you discovered your own wisdom? In the space below, take at least ten minutes to write freely about your innate talents—those abilities that come naturally to you. Alternatively, write freely about the things you've constantly been thinking about (i.e., what the world keeps whispering to you) but haven't yet acted upon.

Intentions

Set your course: Assess the meaningfulness in your life. Examine your relationships, the courses you're taking, and the activities you're involved with right now. How do these pieces of your life provide meaning for you? If they don't ... what do you want to do about it? How will examining these aspects of your life help you move toward your dreams?

_____

_____

_____

_____

_____

_____

_____

_____

_____

_____

_____

_____

_____

_____

_____

_____

*"People say that what we're all seeking is the meaning of life. ...
I think that what we're really seeking is the experience of being alive."*
~ JOSEPH CAMPBELL

Daily intentions: Are you consciously choosing how you spend your time? How so? Do your decisions align with your purpose? Consider any nagging thoughts you have about what you "should" be doing each day. How can you act upon the thoughts that align with your purpose and eliminate the ones that don't?

Discussion and Dialogue

Tap your support system: How have you become more aware of yourself, your talents, your interests, and what matters most to you in life? Ask someone from your support system to help you reflect upon these important questions. What does this person see as your strengths and innate talents? Do his/her observations seem congruent with how you see yourself? Does it matter?

Mapping Your Direction

How have your senses, thoughts, feelings, and intuition influenced your decisions this year? Do you have more clarity? What's still confusing to you? What do you need to do to get where you want to go?

Junior
Year

• JUNIOR YEAR •

Experience

Introduction

Now it's time to put what you've learned so far—about yourself and the world of work—to the test! *Experience* is the focus of your junior year.

Experiencing a career or an industry for yourself is one of the best ways to determine if that career/industry is a good fit for you. While you'll be asked this year to continue some of the academic and experiential activities you've already been working on the last two years, you'll also be challenged to go a step or two further—and take what you've learned out into the real world.

This year, you'll focus on participating in wisely chosen internships, co-op opportunities, service-learning activities, and volunteer activities that will help you build specific skills. Perhaps, for example, you've already been doing a bit of volunteering in college. What have you been *learning* through this activity? Can you continue to grow through this particular experience, or is it time to make a change?

The experiences of your junior year are essential to success in today's increasingly competitive entry-level job market. Whatever you do at this point in your college career should challenge you and help you step out of your comfort zone—for only then will you fully develop the key skills and traits employers are looking for.

You also need to start building your professional skills by learning how to network effectively, doing more *mock interviews* (i.e., practice interviews), attending job/career fairs, gathering letters of reference/recommendation, and perhaps even researching graduate or professional school entrance exams.

You may be tempted to put off some of these activities until senior year. Don't! Too often, college students lose opportunities during the first semester of senior year because they've failed to prepare for those opportunities ahead of time. For example ... the job/career fairs you'll be attending during your senior year—so you can actually try to land a job—often happen in September or October. So you need to do some preparation before that—and junior year is the time to do it!

Academic Activities

• CONTINUING TASKS •

- Strive for a minimum cumulative grade-point average (GPA) of at least 3.0 (on a 4.0 scale). Work particularly hard in your major courses to earn as many A's as you possibly can—B's at a minimum. And if graduate or professional school is in your future, work for an even higher GPA, as close to 4.0 as possible. For better or worse, fairly or unfairly, your grades *do* matter—to both prospective employers and, especially, graduate/professional school admissions personnel.

- Continue meeting with your academic advisor at least twice each semester. When you do, be sure you're taking the courses you're supposed to be taking to complete the various requirements of your major(s) and minor(s). Take the time to be certain *now* so that you're not sorry later!

Choosing Elective Courses

Use your elective credits to take courses that complement your major as well as courses that are *seemingly* unrelated to your major—particularly in the areas of computer applications, foreign languages, communication (written and verbal), and research strategies.

Why

Remember the results of the National Association of Colleges and Employers' annual employer survey on *soft skills*? (If you don't, review this critical information on p. 29 of Freshman Year.) Each year, written and verbal communication skills, analytical skills, and research skills are consistently cited as being among the top traits employers look for when hiring new college graduates. Also consistently high on the list are computer/technical skills and foreign language capabilities.

The more of these skills you can develop while you're in school—particularly through your coursework—the better you'll position yourself with prospective employers, when you're trying to stand out from hundreds of other college students so that you can land the job (or internship/co-op) you really want.

How

1. Talk to other students you know—especially other juniors and some seniors as well—about the elective courses they've taken. What did they like about these classes, and why? Could one or more of these courses be a good fit for your career-related wants/needs?

2. Skim through the *entire* list of courses available at your institution during the upcoming semester and see what titles jump out at you. Write them down and do a little research on the classes that seem most intriguing. For example, you could email the professor who teaches the class you're interested in and ask about it. What will you learn? What is the professor's teaching style? How will this class enrich your life? (Note: This is also a good way to test the professor for this course. Is he/she courteous when you contact him/her? Does he/she give you the

time of day, or does he/she make you feel like you're being a pest? If the latter is true, think very carefully before signing up for a course from this professor.)

3. Look closely at all the course options you have in the area of *communication*—the category employers always rank No. 1 on the list of soft skills they seek in new college graduates—and take at least a few of your electives in this category. If possible, take an elective that taps into one of your strengths so that you can further develop that strength. Alternatively, take a communication course that will help you develop a skill you haven't had much experience with yet.

4. Ask your academic advisor for tips on what elective courses would strengthen the knowledge and skills you're gaining through your major courses—or that would nicely complement that knowledge and those skills.

5. If you can, talk to one or more people who are working in the career you're thinking of pursuing after graduation. What elective courses do *they* recommend that you take, and why? Are such courses available at your school? If so, see if you can fit one or more of them into your schedule.

• ROAD MAP QUESTIONS •

Passions: Is there a discipline you've always wanted to study but never had the chance to? Is there a discipline you know absolutely nothing about through which you could expand your career horizons a bit?

Innate talents: Is there a discipline you've never studied before that you might be good at if you were to give it a try? And are your computer skills, foreign language skills, communication skills, and research skills strong enough for you to be successful in the world of work? How do you know?

_____

_____

_____

_____

_____

_____

What matters most: Is there a discipline you've never studied before that might end up really mattering to you—in your career or in your life in general—if you were to simply give yourself a chance to understand what it's all about?

_____

_____

_____

_____

_____

_____

Getting to Know the Professors

Expand your efforts to get to know your professors so that, by the end of this year, two or three professors know you well enough to speak highly of your academic (and perhaps out-of-class) achievements—in the form of a letter of reference, for example, or willingness to talk to prospective employers or (graduate/professional school personnel) about you.

Why

Professors who know you well will be more motivated to write a good reference letter for you and help you in your future job search in other ways (e.g., introducing you to prospective employers they know, telling you about job openings they hear about). Indeed, professors who know you well are very often your first *networking* contacts, who can play a vital role in helping you get your career off to a good start.

How

1. Which classes do you do especially well in? Which ones intrigue you the most because of their subject matter? The professors of these courses are ones you should get to know because they already have something in common with you—a shared passion for the discipline in which they teach. So stop by during your professors' office hours and share a little about what you're hoping to do with your life. Ask for their advice on how to get the most out of their courses and how to learn more about what they're teaching. Most professors enjoy helping students who are clearly and sincerely self-motivated—and not just because they want to earn a good grade in a course.

2. Ask your favorite professor if you can take him/her out for coffee on campus sometime to learn more about how he/she found his career. (Note: Some colleges/universities have special funds set aside that students and/or professors can use to pay for these coffee sessions [or even lunches or dinners together!] because they want to actively encourage out-of-class interactions between students and professors. Does *your* school have this type of program? Have you checked?)

3. Once you've begun developing a good relationship with a particular professor, keep him/her in the loop when, for example, you're applying for internships or jobs. Ask him/her—ahead of time—if he/she would

serve as a reference for you with prospective employers (or graduate/ professional schools).

4. Make sure you sincerely acknowledge your professor(s) by sending a brief email or card of thanks for anything he/she does for you. Not only is this common (but too often overlooked) courtesy; it's also a way of ensuring that your professor will *continue* offering his/her help to you in the future. (After all ... when you thank someone for his/her efforts, he/she is more likely to continue putting forth such efforts.)

• ROAD MAP QUESTIONS •

Passions: Is there a professor you know who is so passionate about his/her discipline that you can't help but become passionate about it yourself? Who is that professor, and what is it about his/her subject area that intrigues you so?

_____

_____

_____

_____

_____

_____

_____

_____

_____

_____

_____

_____

Innate talents: Have you gotten to know at least one professor who can speak intelligently and accurately about your abilities and skills—in a letter of recommendation, for example, or in discussions with prospective employers or graduate/professional schools?

_____

_____

_____

_____

_____

_____

What matters most: Is there a professor who has gotten to know you well enough to understand what really makes you tick—that is, what you value (in life and in work) and how you want to carry out what you value in your day-to-day activities? Does this professor understand what really drives you? If so, how might this professor help you a) envision a future career, and b) grab the attention of prospective employers or graduate/professional schools?

_____

_____

_____

_____

_____

_____

_____

Research Courses and Independent Study Seminars

Take a research course or an independent study seminar that allows you to complete a major research project (i.e., a *thesis*) on a topic of very strong interest to you.

Why

Developing solid writing skills is essential no matter which career path you ultimately pursue. In fact, in the annual *soft skills* survey conducted by the National Association of Colleges and Employers (see p. 129 of Freshman Year), employers consistently cite communication (written and verbal) as the *No. 1* soft skill they look for in college students and recent college graduates. By researching and writing a major paper, or *thesis*, you'll be able to not merely *say* you have strong writing skills, but *prove* it. (Big difference!)

But that's not the only reason you should complete a complex research project during your time as an undergraduate. Doing so will also:

- Give you hands-on experience in conducting research as well as studying the research findings of others. Employers consistently rate research skills as high on the list of soft skills they seek in college students and recent grads.

- Allow you to develop some expertise on a topic you enjoy studying—a topic that may well be part of your career someday. What better way to shine in a job interview than to be able to quote the findings of your own research on a specific issue or problem in your chosen field?

- Help you develop a solid connection with, for example, a professor who advises you on your research project, and/or an off-campus professional who helps you carry it out (e.g., your internship supervisor who allows you to conduct a survey of all the interns in the company).

How

1. If your institution or academic department *requires* the completion of an intensive research project/thesis, sign up to begin on that task starting this, your junior, year.

2. Most academic departments offer an Independent Study (or similarly-named) course each semester, through which you can complete a

research project for an agreed-upon number of credits. Look for these courses in various departments that interest you and see if you can arrange an Independent Study in collaboration with a professor(s) in one of those departments.

3. Ask a few of your professors if they know of any research needs within their departments. (Example: The psychology department would like to know why so many students do poorly in its "Abnormal Psychology" course.) Perhaps you could be an essential part of uncovering some answers!

4. Some schools have an Undergraduate Research Opportunities Program (UROP) designed for undergraduates who want to complete major research activities. This type of initiative is another option you can look into. (Note: You may even be paid for your work through a program of this type.)

5. Approach a student affairs professional on campus and ask him/her if the student affairs division could use any research help (from you!). Perhaps, for instance, your school is seeing too many students leave after their freshman year and wants to know what's going on. Your research project could help the school find out.

6. Take an hour sometime to go sit in a quiet place and think about the many "why" questions you likely have now that you're in your junior year of college. Possible examples: "Why do colleges and universities spend so much money on athletics?" "Why are so many political advertisements so negative?" "Why do the heads of major companies so often commit criminal offenses related to company finances?" What do you naturally wonder about in your life? Perhaps one of these topics—if you can focus it a bit with the help of a faculty advisor—would make for an excellent major research project.

• ROAD MAP QUESTIONS •

Passions: Which disciplines and topics interest you so much that you want to learn about them in great depth? What do you find yourself reading about (or watching on TV or listening to on the radio) just for its own sake (i.e., not because you have to for a class)?

_____

_____

_____

Innate talents: Can you handle the difficult tasks involved in developing, executing, and writing up the results of a major research project? Do you have conceptualization skills? research and interviewing skills? strong written and verbal communication skills? Additionally, do you have a natural curiosity about a certain topic(s)? If so, do you have enough drive to devote significant time and energy to studying it?

_____

_____

_____

What matters most: What problems and issues in life truly need addressing, in your opinion? What, in your view, are the needs of the world and the big questions that need to be answered? What topics do you feel so strongly about that you find it impossible to ignore them or brush them aside?

_____

_____

_____

Career Development Courses

Take a course on career development and/or the job search process, and work hard to do well in it—not just for the grade but for your personal benefit as well.

Why

By taking a career development and/or job search course, you can work on many of the same tasks you're completing throughout this book—but in a more formal way, and under the guidance of a career development expert. The course will also force you to meet certain deadlines for various activities—a good benefit if you tend to otherwise put things off, no matter how helpful they might be to you. (It's one thing to say, "I'll put together a resumé ... sometime"; it's quite another to say, "I need to have my resumé done for class by the end of the day on Friday.")

How

1. See if your academic department or school/college offers a career development course for students in your major or school/college. If it does, register for the course as soon as you can.

2. If your academic department or school/college does *not* offer a career development course, contact your institution's career center and see if *it* offers a career development course (for credit). If it does, register for the course as soon as you can.

3. If you can't find a for-credit career development course anywhere at your school, see if your institution's career center offers shorter, non-credit seminars or mini-courses on career development and/or job search strategies. If it does, attend one or more of these seminars or mini-courses as soon as you can.

4. Consider taking a career development or job search course via online/distance education—either through your own institution or another.

5. Consider taking a career development or job search course through your institution's college/school of Continuing Education—or through the Continuing Education department of another nearby college or university. (You don't necessarily have to take a career course at *your* institution to gain the knowledge you need.)

6. Another possibility is to take a career development or job search course at an institution near where you live during the summer months.

• ROAD MAP QUESTIONS •

Passions: Is your career development/job search course helping you gauge what your strongest interests are? Conversely, is it giving you a good idea of what you *don't* enjoy (which can be as critical as knowing what you *do* enjoy!)? What fields/industries intrigue you at this point? How do you know? Have you gained this knowledge from a career assessment like the Strong Interest Inventory? from an experiential activity like an informational interview? from a book or web site you read to research a certain career area?

Innate talents: Is your career development/job search course helping you better understand what you're naturally good at (i.e., innate talents)? Is it helping you pinpoint the skills you've learned over the years through various educational and work experiences? Which of your abilities and skills are the most fun for you to use? the least fun? (Remember: It's one thing to be *good at* something; it's quite another to *enjoy doing* that something!)

_____

_____

_____

_____

_____

What matters most: Is your career development/job search course helping you gain a better sense of what really matters to you in life—especially in your future career? Are you learning, for example, where you stand in relation to key work-related values like job security, salary, and power? How about other key values like independence, creativity, and decision making? What will you *refuse to tolerate* in your future career? What will make you want to jump out of bed each morning and be excited to go to work?

_____

_____

_____

_____

_____

_____

Experiential Activities

• CONTINUING TASKS •

- Continue collecting items for your *career portfolio*, and have your portfolio done by at least mid-year so you can use it in interviews with employers. (see tips for doing so in this section, p. 144)

- Continue researching careers in more depth by not only reading about them, but also talking (in person or via phone/email) to people who actually work in them (i.e., *informational interviewing*—see p. 97 of Sophomore Year).

- Continue researching companies and organizations you might want to work for someday (see p. 104 of Sophomore Year).

• NEW TASKS •

Seeking a Leadership Role in a Campus Organization

Take on a high(er)-level leadership role in at least one campus organization.

Why

If you got into a lower-level leadership position in a student group during your sophomore year, wonderful! Now it's time to continue your growth by pursuing a higher-level position—such as being an officer (e.g., treasurer, vice president, president) in the organization.

Why? Several reasons:

- Employers who hire new college graduates consistently report that they're looking for grads who have *leadership* skills and experience. (Revisit the results of the *soft skills* survey of employers conducted annually by the National Association of Colleges and Employers—see p. 29 of Freshman Year). Leading a student group is a natural way for you to get that experience and develop sound leadership abilities.

- Often, as a high-level leader of a campus organization, you get to know—on a personal basis—several key faculty members on campus (among them your group's faculty advisor); key members of the student affairs staff on campus; and, on occasion, local professionals/ employers in your group's area of focus. The people in all three of these broad groups might someday provide solid references for you. Just as important, they'll likely pass along internship and/or job leads to you as they hear about them. (After all, if they see you in action as a strong leader on campus, why *wouldn't* they make you aware of ways to do the same thing off campus?)

- As a high-level leader in a campus organization, you'll almost certainly be compelled to learn (or polish) skills in essential areas like budgeting and financial management, recruiting, marketing and public relations, team building, communication (written and verbal), and fundraising. Expertise in just one of these areas (let alone several) will, by itself, make you stand out in relation to most other college students and recent graduates. (If *you* were an employer, wouldn't you be more likely to hire a student who *has* these skills and experiences vs. a student who *does not have* them?)

How

1. Look critically at the campus organization(s) you're involved in and identify where more (or better) leadership is needed. If no leadership position exists to address that area(s), volunteer to take on that role yourself. Conversely, if addressing that area(s) requires you to be in a high-level leadership position within the organization, put your name in for consideration.

2. As you consider high-level leadership positions that are filled by new people each school year, examine your own strengths and interests. Will you be most effective—and will you have a more rewarding experience—if you're the president of the group? Or are you a better fit for a different high-level position, such as treasurer, vice president, secretary, fundraising chairperson, or recruiting chairperson?

3. Talk to people who hold (or have held) high-level leadership positions in your student group. What do they like about their jobs? What do they dislike? Where do they see you fitting in best when it comes to a high-level leadership role? Might one of them serve as a sort of mentor to you as you seek to land a high-level leadership position in the organization?

• ROAD MAP QUESTIONS •

Passions: Do you enjoy leading a group from a big-picture standpoint—i.e., as a high-level officer, who worries less about day-to-day details and more about the overall direction of the organization? Or do you prefer leading at a lower, more grassroots level where you have more of a chance to get your hands dirty? How might this knowledge affect you in, say, your first job after you graduate from college?

· ROAD MAP QUESTIONS ·

Innate talents: Are you a born leader? If so, how do you know? If not, are you starting to *learn* sound leadership skills? How do you know?

_____

_____

_____

_____

_____

What matters most: Is it important for you to take a strong leadership role in the activities/issues that matter to you, or would you prefer to be a strong follower or colleague instead? Do you want (need?) to run the zoo, or are you content with simply working *at* the zoo? (Or is the truth somewhere in between—i.e., do you prefer a mid-level leadership role?)

_____

_____

_____

_____

_____

_____

_____

Revising Your Resumé

Revise your resumé to reflect the experiences, skills, and accomplishments you gained during sophomore year and the summer following sophomore year.

Why

By this time in your academic career, your resumé is probably going to look vastly different from the first draft you developed freshman year. That's good—because as you've already come to know (hopefully!), a resumé is a living document that needs to change as you change and grow. It would be foolish for you to continue using the same resumé you wrote freshman year. After all, you almost certainly have more experiences, skills, and accomplishments to brag about now vs. a couple of years ago. How will an employer ever know about them if you don't revise your resumé?

How

1. Make an appointment with a counselor at your school's career center and let him/her know that you'd like to spend your time together revising your resumé.

2. Before your appointment, take three sheets of paper and—just as you did last year for this same purpose—label them "New Experiences," "New Skills," and "New Accomplishments," respectively.

3. Take your "New Experiences" sheet and start jotting down any new experiences you can think of that have occurred between your sophomore year and now. *Do not limit yourself at this point!* If something jumps into your mind—no matter how minor or insignificant it might seem— write it down! The idea is to do a "brain dump" and get everything out of your head and onto paper. Later, you and your career counselor can decide what to add to your resumé and what to leave off.

4. Go through the same "brain dump" exercise with your "New Skills" and "New Accomplishments" sheets. Again, *do not limit yourself at this point!*

5. Once you've finished writing down everything you can think of on each of these sheets, keep them in a handy spot ... just in case you think of other entries to add later.

6. Bring the sheets to your appointment with your career counselor and tell him/her you've written down everything you can think of. Ask him/her to help you remember anything you may have forgotten or disregarded.

7. With the counselor's help, decide which entries to add to your resumé and which to leave off. As was the case last year, you'll almost certainly have to do some reformatting of your resumé to accommodate the changes—that's par for the course.

8. Once you've finished revising your resumé, set up another appointment and ask your career counselor to look at it one last time for minor revisions.

• ROAD MAP QUESTIONS •

Passions: Does your revised resumé reflect what you're passionate about—especially any new topics/issues/concerns you've *become* passionate about in the last year or so? How do you know?

_____

_____

_____

_____

_____

_____

_____

_____

_____

• ROAD MAP QUESTIONS •

Innate talents: Does your revised resumé highlight the new skills and experiences you've gained over the last year or so? Are they easy for the reader to quickly spot? How do you know? Have you been specific about these achievements, and have you quantified them wherever possible (e.g., "Increased group membership by 20%")?

_____

_____

_____

_____

_____

What matters most: Does your revised resumé clearly illustrate what you represent and what matters most to you? Is it easy for the reader to quickly spot this essential information? If the reader had just ten seconds to look at your resumé (not an unrealistic possibility, by the way!), would he/she be able to get a basic sense of who you are and what you're about? Are you sure?

_____

_____

_____

_____

_____

_____

The Career Portfolio

Create a *career portfolio* highlighting your accomplishments and skills.

Why

Every day, employers interview job applicants who *tell* those employers about their skills and experiences—"I can do this," "I can do that." If you talk to any employers, you'll soon realize that there's a problem with this scenario: Applicants can (and often do) *say anything* in job interviews, sometimes stretching the truth and—more often than you'd like to think—telling outright lies to employers.

"Upper management is raising the performance bar at all levels, and hiring managers want to interview and hire only candidates who specifically have the skill sets, talents, and motivations that match the job qualifications. They're almost shouting, 'Show me the proof you have exactly what I'm looking for!'"

~ RICK NELLES,
NATIONAL DIRECTOR OF COLLEGE
RECRUITING FOR THE PRINCETON
SEARCH GROUP AND AUTHOR OF
PROOF OF PERFORMANCE:
HOW TO BUILD A CAREER PORTFOLIO
TO LAND A GREAT NEW JOB

Sad? Yes. True? Yes.

That's why most employers today are looking for *evidence* that you can do what you *say* you can do, and that you've really done what you *say* you've done. You can provide that evidence—and then some—by developing a *career portfolio* and using it in your job and internship interviews.

A career portfolio is simply a professional-looking, three-ring binder in which you can display tangible evidence of your past accomplishments and current skills. For example: It's one thing to mention an award you've won on your resume; but you'll make more of an impact on a prospective employer if you can show him/her a picture of you receiving the award, as well as the actual award itself. All of it can be on display in your career portfolio.

What you include in your portfolio is limited only by your imagination. You might display excellent papers you've written, publications you've developed, honors you've received, photos of activities you've been involved in, letters of recommendation or congratulations you've received, highlights of interesting class projects you've completed, and much more.

In doing so, you'll be among the few job applicants who can *show* an employer what you have to offer—not just *talk about it.*

There's a more intangible (but no less important) benefit too, especially if you anticipate job interviews being nerve-wracking experiences: If you have a portfolio in hand, you have a "prop" of sorts that you can use to more effectively tell the employer about yourself and your achievements. You can use your portfolio to do a mini show-and-tell of your skills and accomplishments—which is generally much easier than recalling everything from memory and then trying to recite it to the employer.

You just can't go wrong by developing a career portfolio for yourself. On the contrary, a portfolio will boost your confidence and improve your job interview performance.

How

1. Go to your campus bookstore or a nearby office supply store and buy a *nice* three-ring binder. (This isn't the time to be frugal and buy one of the $2.99 variety. Spend $20 instead and get a good binder that will look professional—and that will last.)

2. Additionally, buy some section dividers for the binder, along with some clear plastic display pages (with hole punches on the side) and some labeling tabs (with labels). You'll use all of these materials to create various sections for your portfolio, and to then label those sections and fill each one with the clear plastic pages (where your actual materials will be displayed).

3. Find the box in which you've been saving your future career portfolio materials the last couple of years. (Note: If you haven't been saving materials in a special place, start gathering materials together now. Put them in a box or some other container where they'll all be in one place.)

4. Look at the materials you have and start sorting them into four or five basic categories. Some possibilities: "Academics," "Student Activities," "Volunteer Activities," "Awards/Honors," "Work/Internships," "Leadership Experience," "Communication Skills." There is no one "right" way

to do this! Just make your best attempt to organize your materials in a way that will make sense to someone else who looks at your portfolio (i.e., a prospective employer).

5. Once you've finished developing your basic organizational scheme, use the labeling tabs and section dividers you bought to create the main sections of your portfolio. Within each of these sections, put in a few clear plastic display pages.

6. Go ahead and put your materials into the plastic display pages, each in the appropriate section.

7. If you want to, use a word processing program to create brief captions for each of your portfolio items. Example: "Receiving the Outstanding Leader award from University of Arizona President Judy Jones, April 30, 2006." (Note: Not only will these captions help the person who is reading your portfolio; they'll also help *you* as you talk about the various items during your interviews.)

8. If you get stuck during any part of the portfolio development process, get some help from a counselor at your school's career center, your academic advisor, or other students you know who have created portfolios themselves. Alternatively, you can consult one of several useful books on career portfolios:

- *The Career Portfolio Workbook*, by Frank Satterthwaite and Gary D'Orsi (published by McGraw-Hill, 2002)

- *Creating Your Career Portfolio: At a Glance Guide for Students*, by Anna Graf Williams and Karen J. Hall (published by Prentice Hall, 2004)

- *Proof of Performance: How to Build a Career Portfolio to Land a Great New Job*, by Rick Nelles (published by Impact Publications, 2000)

• ROAD MAP QUESTIONS •

Passions: As you look through your completed (for now!) career portfolio, do you get the sense that someone reading through it (i.e., a prospective employer) will be able to see evidence of what your strongest interests and passions are? If not, what materials can you add to your portfolio to make your passions/interests stand out more effectively?

_____

_____

_____

_____

_____

_____

Innate talents: Will someone reading through your portfolio (i.e., a prospective employer) see some proof of your key abilities and skills? Have you considered showing your portfolio to someone who doesn't know you very well and asking him/her to tell you what abilities and skills he/she sees evidence of in your portfolio? What feedback do you think you'll get?

_____

_____

_____

_____

_____

_____

What matters most: Will someone reading through your portfolio (i.e., a prospective employer) get a good idea of what's most important to you—especially in your work and career-related activities? How do you know?

_____

_____

_____

_____

Networking

Begin _networking_—starting with people you already know and then moving to people you don't know (yet!)—so you can get to know people (and they you) in various organizations and industries.

Why

Networking is, by far, the best way to learn about careers and organizations. After all, who better to tell you about a career or company than someone who is actually working _in_ that career or company?

Just as important, networking is the most efficient and effective way for you to find a job when you graduate—or even an internship or a co-op while you're still in school. If you put yourself in the shoes of an employer, it's easy to understand why.

Imagine you're an employer and you need to hire someone for a job or an internship. More than likely, your own job is on the line—in some ways, at least—because you need to make a good hiring decision. (If you don't, your bad hire will cost the organization money in the form of wasted salary, wasted time, and wasted effort—and your own supervisor will thus be displeased with you.) Moreover, if you're like many professionals, you've already been burned at least once by a job candidate who made lots of great-sounding claims in the interview but didn't live up to any of them on the job.

So you're naturally cautious. You're a bit skeptical. And you certainly aren't going to hire just anyone for this job.

What can you do to minimize your risks? One of two things:

- Interview and hire someone you already know very well—someone you can trust because he/she has proven himself/herself trustworthy to you in the past.

- Interview and hire someone who comes highly recommended by someone you know and trust—after all, if someone you trust can vouch for this person, the candidate must be a good risk.

Now you know why networking—starting now—is so critical to your job or internship search(es) later. By networking now, you become a known quantity to prospective employers. And employers will always hire a known quantity over an unknown quantity. It's faster, it's easier, it's almost always cheaper, and—most crucial of all—it's decidedly less risky.

How

1. Start your networking efforts by first talking to people in your own life instead of total strangers. You'd be surprised at the expertise and connections that are right in your own circle of acquaintances. For example, you could talk to neighbors, parents of your college or high school friends, former teachers, and even people your parents or relatives know. Ask them about their careers and their places of employment. Do they know about any internships or jobs that might be a good fit for you? Are they willing to simply keep their eyes open and contact you if they hear about any such internships or jobs? (Note: More than likely, they *are* willing; but they won't know to contact you unless and until you ask!)

2. If you prefer communicating in writing versus in person, you can network by emailing people who are in careers/industries of interest and asking them questions. Or you could use email to introduce yourself and then invite the person you've contacted out for a face-to-face conversation over coffee.

3. One of the easiest and most effective—but too often overlooked or discounted—ways you can network as a college student is to join and get involved in a professional organization in your field of interest. In many

cases, professional organizations have campus chapters and/or local chapters you can join—typically for a very low cost if you're a current college student. If you then simply start attending the regular meetings of your campus and/or local chapter, you'll start getting to know people in your field—and giving them a chance to get to know you.

4. Whenever you talk to a networking contact, focus on asking for just two things: information and advice. You don't want to make people feel like you're simply hitting them up for a job. So instead, just ask for *information* and *advice*—both of which anyone can readily and easily provide. You'll still get the feedback you need; but you'll do so in a way that doesn't make your networking contact want to run away from you!

5. Consider developing a one-page *leave-behind paper* highlighting your key interests/passions, abilities and skills, personality traits, and career goals. You can then carry copies of this document with you—instead of or in addition to your resumé—each time you meet with a new networking contact face to face. Give a copy of your leave-behind paper to all the people you talk to—so that they can easily remember you weeks or months from now, and perhaps pass your information on to other contacts.

6. Every time you talk with new networking contacts, ask them if they know of other people you should talk to—and if they will help you connect with these other people by, for example, making an introductory phone call or sending an introductory email on your behalf. At a minimum, ask each new networking contact if you can "namedrop" his/her name to the next person you try to contact. For example: "I spoke with Jane Smith the other day, and she suggested I contact you." It's always a little easier to find a new networking contact when you can say you were referred by someone that person already knows.

7. After each chat you have with a new networking contact, send him/her a quick thank-you note. It's common courtesy, for starters. But it will also help you stand out in that person's mind as a conscientious, professional person who is worthy of being helped.

• ROAD MAP QUESTIONS •

Passions: As you talk to various people through your networking efforts, which of them are engaged in day-to-day activities that really grab your interest? What are these activities that you find so inherently fascinating, and why do you like them so much?

_____

_____

_____

_____

_____

Innate talents: How are your "people" skills? Can you make people feel comfortable talking with you, and are you comfortable talking with them? If not, how can you improve this essential skill? Additionally, are the people you're networking with giving you a better sense of where you might best put your favorite talents and skills to good use? Do you see any patterns in the feedback you're getting?

_____

_____

_____

_____

_____

_____

THE COLLEGE TO CAREER ROAD MAP

What matters most: Among the people you network with, who seems really satisfied with their work, and why? Are there any people who seem unhappy with their work? What seems to make them so dissatisfied? Do you see any patterns?

_____

_____

_____

_____

_____

Utilizing Mock Interviews

Ask a campus career counselor to do some additional *mock interviews* with you so you can hone your presentation skills in preparation for real job or internship interviews.

Why

When (if?) you participated in *mock interviews* (i.e., practice interviews) during your sophomore year (see p. 107 of Sophomore Year), you no doubt discovered how valuable they are in helping you get ready for real interviews. Well, this year you're going to start *having* real interviews—for internships and/or jobs—so practicing some more, ahead of time, will help you prepare to do your very best.

Remember: Employers will be expecting you to do a solid job of presenting your skills, education, and experiences in an interview situation. They'll want you to carry yourself well and back up your statements with solid evidence. Sound stressful? It is! That's why practicing with a career counselor—and discussing your performance immediately afterward—is so critical.

How

1. Set up a mock interview appointment with your career counselor at the school's career center. If possible, arrange for your mock interview to be videotaped (or at least audiotaped) so that you can watch (or listen to) yourself afterward and critique your performance with the help of your counselor.

2. Get your resumé into your career counselor's hands a few days before your mock interview so that he/she can prepare for the discussion in advance.

3. Choose a specific job at a specific company to "interview" for and let your career counselor know, ahead of time, what that job and company will be. That way, your counselor can develop specific questions that align closely with the questions you'll potentially be asked during a real interview with that company.

4. To the degree possible, prepare for your mock interview just as you'd prepare for a real interview. Research the organization and jot down some questions you can ask during the discussion.

5. On the day of your mock interview, dress just as you would for the real thing. (That way your counselor can evaluate not only your interview performance but your attire and "look" as well.)

6. Once your mock interview is done, debrief with your counselor immediately. Start by telling the counselor what *you* think you did well and not so well. Then ask the counselor for his/her insights. The *feedback* you receive after a mock interview is the most important reason for doing a mock interview in the first place! So don't just interview and run.

• ROAD MAP QUESTIONS •

Passions: When you start having real interviews, will you be able to truly *demonstrate* your interest in a) your chosen field, b) the organization you're interviewing with, and c) the job at hand? How will you *prove* your interest to often skeptical employers—most of whom have been burned at least once by interviewees who claimed things in an interview but didn't live up to those claims on the job?

Innate talents: Are you prepared to effectively describe your abilities and skills in response to the various types of questions employers will likely ask you—*general* (e.g., "Tell me about yourself"), *situational* (e.g., "What would you do if ____?"), and *behavioral* (e.g., "Tell me about a time in the past when you had to ____.")?

_____

_____

_____

_____

_____

_____

_____

_____

What matters most: Can you effectively tell prospective employers what's important to you in your work, in the organization you work *for*, and in the people you work *with*?

_____

_____

_____

_____

_____

_____

_____

_____

Professional Organizations Related to Career Choice

Join and get involved in at least one professional organization related to your chosen major and/or career.

Why

College students who are involved in professional organizations tend to highly impress the professional members of those organizations. By being in a professional organization as a student, you not only *say* you're committed to your field of interest, you *demonstrate* it.

Put yourself in the shoes of a prospective employer. You're interviewing a couple of new college graduates for an entry-level newspaper reporting job. One of the candidates has been an active student member of the local Society of Professional Journalists (SPJ) chapter for the last two years. (You know this for a fact because you've seen the candidate yourself at many of the SPJ meetings.) The other candidate has no involvement with SPJ or any other journalism- or communication-related professional group.

Which of these new-grad candidates is likely more committed to and focused on newspaper journalism as a career? The evidence strongly suggests it's the first candidate—thanks in no small part to his involvement in a professional organization.

How

1. If you're involved in a campus organization on campus, see if it has a connection with an outside professional organization—at the local level, the state level, or even the national level. If it does, visit the web site of this larger, outside professional group and see how you can join and get involved. (Note: In many cases, professional groups at all levels offer college student memberships that cost a mere fraction of what typical professional dues cost.)

2. Talk to professors and fellow students in your academic department and ask them about professional organizations they're aware of that might be a good fit for you. Visit the web sites of the suggested groups and see if any of them will be of professional benefit to you.

3. Use an Internet search tool like Google (www.google.com) or Yahoo! (www.yahoo.com) to search for professional associations in your field(s) of interest.

4. Go to your campus or local public library and ask a reference librarian there to show you the print or online version of the *Encyclopedia of Associations* (or a similar resource) so you can search for professional organizations by topic area or geographic area.

5. Once you find a professional organization to join, do so—and, if possible, start attending its regular meetings at the local level. (You can find announcements of those meetings on the organization's web site—or, in many cases, in the business section of your local daily newspaper.) It's one thing to simply receive a professional group's publications or use its web site resources; but you'll benefit even more by getting to know some of the actual *people* in the organization face to face—and helping them get to know you.

• ROAD MAP QUESTIONS •

Passions: What are the people in your new professional organization doing in their careers that excites you? What about the organization's publications grabs your interest? How about its conferences?

_____

_____

_____

Innate talents: As you interact with people in your new professional organization and read its publications, what are you learning about the key abilities and skills that seem to be critical in this field?

_____

_____

_____

_____

What matters most: What seems to matter most to the people in your new professional organization? How well do these values match up with your own—especially where your future career is concerned?

_____

_____

_____

_____

Job/Career Fairs

Familiarize yourself with the job/career fair environment by attending at least one job/career fair, on or off campus.

Why

It won't be long until you embark on an extensive search for a full-time job. One of the many ways you can do just that is to attend a job/career fair, where prospective employers come together in one place—usually a large auditorium of some sort, either on campus or off—to recruit prospective employees.

Making the most of a job/career fair is part science, part art. You need to learn how to effectively approach the employers in attendance, introduce yourself, and—perhaps most difficult of all—talk about yourself and the education, skills, and experiences you have to offer. It can be exciting, yes; but it can also be intimidating and nerve-wracking, at least in the beginning.

So why not simply plan on *attending* a job/career fair during this, your junior, year so that you can observe a bit? Get used to the feel of the atmosphere. Eavesdrop on a few conversations between students and employers. Which students seem to be doing the best, and what exactly are they doing to make themselves stand out?

Just as important, what do the employers in attendance seem to be asking about or looking for consistently?

Jot down a few notes on what you see and hear so you'll have something to refer back to the next time you attend a job/career fair—when you'll probably really be competing with the rest of the attendees to land a job.

How

1. Early in the school year, stop by your school's career center or visit its web site to get a sense of what on- and off-campus job/career fairs will be offered in your geographic area in the coming months. (Note: Sometimes you have to sign up in advance if you want to attend a particular fair—so be sure to follow any requirements that have been set out by the career center and/or the sponsoring organization[s] of the fair.)

2. Keep an eye on the career section of the local newspaper (or its web site). Often, local job/career fairs are sponsored by—or at least publicized by—newspapers as a service to readers.

3. Stop by any local government or nonprofit agencies that focus on career issues (e.g., a local workforce center, a nonprofit career counseling agency)—or visit their web sites—to keep abreast of upcoming job/career fairs in your area.

4. Once you choose a job/career fair to attend, prepare a few copies of your resumé to bring with you ... just in case you run into an employer who would like a copy (or to whom you'd like to *give* a copy!).

5. Dress appropriately for the fair you attend. Usually, *business casual* dress—somewhere between shorts-and-flip-flops and suit-and-tie—is appropriate. If in doubt, you're far better off being *over*dressed versus *under*dressed!

6. When you arrive at the job/career fair, check in at the registration table, pick up any materials that are being handed out, and put on a name tag if one is offered to you.

7. Start walking around the job/career fair, listening and observing. Get a feel for the event. How are people acting and interacting?

8. Look for employer tables/areas that are surrounded by lots of attendees. Pick one and go over by the other attendees so you can observe and listen if you'd like, yet blend in at the same time. Give yourself a chance to learn vicariously—through the words and actions of others.

9. If you want to, talk to an employer or two before you leave. If you see an employer you're *really* interested in, stop and talk to a *different*, less-interesting employer first. Give yourself the opportunity to practice under less pressure!

10. If/when you talk to an employer, be sure to ask for his/her card before you go—and leave a copy of your resumé with him/her too.

11. Within twenty-four hours after the job/career fair is over, send or email a thank-you note to the employer(s) you spoke with at the fair. You'll stand out for this simple but too-often-ignored act of gratitude.

• ROAD MAP QUESTIONS •

Passions: During your time at the job/career fair and in your reflection shortly thereafter, what specific companies/organizations really got you pumped up? Why? Which of the companies/organizations offer products, services, or causes that truly excite you? What's so interesting about these products/services/causes?

Innate talents: When you were at the job/career fair, did you come upon any companies/organizations that could potentially tap some of your best (and favorite) abilities and skills? What sorts of things could you do for this organization? Where might its needs match up with your talents? How could you someday market your key abilities and skills to this organization?

_____

_____

_____

_____

_____

_____

_____

What matters most: At the job/career fair, did you learn about any companies/organizations whose products, services, or causes might be a good fit with what's most important to you in life? Moreover, did you find out about any organizations where your career would bring you the rewards _you_ want—be it a high salary, job security, work/life balance, great co-workers, or whatever?

_____

_____

_____

_____

_____

_____

Researching Graduate/Professional School Programs

If applicable, start researching graduate/professional programs and preparing to take entrance exams (e.g., GRE, GMAT, LSAT, MCAT).

Why

Start this process now if you plan to attend graduate or professional school. Why? So you don't miss any critical deadlines.

You should also decide if you want/need to attend graduate/professional school right after you finish your undergraduate degree or instead work for a year or two and then attend. Some graduate/professional school programs—particularly MBA programs—prefer or even require that you get some real-world experience to be considered for admission.

How

1. Set up an appointment with a counselor at your school's career center. Let him/her know that you want to research graduate/professional schools and learn more about the process of applying to them.

2. Go to your campus or local bookstore and page through some of the many books available on graduate/professional school and how to get in. (Note: These books are published by companies like Peterson's and Princeton Review.)

3. Visit web sites like Peterson's (www.petersons.com) and Princeton Review (www.princetonreview.com) to find additional information on graduate/professional schools and how to get into the program of your choice.

4. Each graduate/professional school program you come across will have criteria that list the minimum admission requirements (e.g., GPA, entrance exam scores, courses taken) as well as the program's averages for GPA and entrance exam scores. Look for this information; it will give you a good idea of how well a particular program might fit you (or not fit you, as the case may be).

5. Preparation programs for graduate school entrance exams are widely available—sometimes right on campus but more typically off campus via private companies and self-study programs (e.g., books, computer programs, videos). Assess whether or not you have the discipline to

prepare for your graduate/professional school exam(s) on your own. Will the structure and expertise offered by a preparation program be worth the cost? Why or why not?

6. Ask your professors and other trusted adults in your life if it would be better for you to go to graduate/professional school right away or instead to get some real-world experience first. Be sure to talk to people who have a wide variety of perspectives!

• ROAD MAP QUESTIONS •

Passions: What graduate/professional school programs interest you the most? What can you see yourself studying for the next two to five years or more? Why?

_____

_____

_____

_____

Innate talents: In which graduate/professional school programs are you most likely to be successful from an academic standpoint? Additionally, will you be able to do well enough on any graduate/professional school entrance exam(s) you'll need to take? How do you know? Might you need to invest in a test-preparation program of some sort, on or off campus? Why or why not?

_____

_____

_____

_____

What matters most: What graduate/professional school programs will help you prepare for the life you want to live after graduation (whatever that may entail!)? How do you know?

_____

_____

_____

_____

_____

Skill-Building Experiences

The Value of Internships

Complete at least one internship or co-op experience during your junior year (or the summer immediately following junior year).

Why

Given today's increasingly competitive entry-level job market, doing an internship or co-op is no longer *optional* for college students; in employers' minds, it's *essential* experience for you to obtain while you're in school.

(Just how important is internship or co-op experience? Consider the eye-opening research findings on the following page.)

You simply must—*must*—get some experience through an internship or a co-op before you graduate. If you don't, you'll struggle to keep up with the thousands of other college students and recent grads who *do* have internship/co-op experience

How

1. If you've been tracking internship/co-op possibilities in an "Internship/Co-op Possibilities" binder since your sophomore year (see p. 101 of Sophomore Year), great! Now is the time to return to that binder and make some decisions about which opportunities you'd like to pursue.

• FACT •

Employers offer full-time, permanent jobs to 58 percent of the students who do internships with their organizations and 60 percent of the students who do co-ops with their organizations, according to the 2004 Experiential Education Survey conducted by the National Association of Colleges and Employers (a trade association for college/university career services professionals and employers who hire new college graduates).

Why these high numbers of interns-turned-employees? Because these students have already proven themselves to their respective employers—and employers will hire proven experience over unproven lack of experience every single time.

2. If, on the other hand, you're just beginning to research internship or co-op possibilities, here are several specific ways to go about it:

- Visit your school's career center (or its web site) and check out the internship and co-op listings it has obtained from various organizations.

- Check out a college-oriented career web site like MonsterTRAK (www.monstertrak.com), Experience (www.experience.com), College Grad (www.collegegrad.com), or CollegeRecruiter (www.collegerecruiter.com) and look for internship and co-op listings there.

- Go to your campus library or a nearby bookstore and look through one of the many printed internship directories that are on the market (published by companies like Princeton Review and Peterson's). (Note: At the bookstore, you'll find such guides in the "Careers" or "College Guides" section.)

- Talk to your professors and fellow students and ask them where current and previous students from your school/department have done internships or co-ops in the past. (Note: Employers often prefer hiring new interns or co-op students from the same schools/departments where they've had success doing so in the past. Take advantage of this phenomenon!)

- Talk to a counselor at your school's career center (particularly if the center has an *internship coordinator* or similarly titled person on staff). Ask him/her where previous students from your school have interned or done co-ops in the past.

- Directly approach any organizations that interest you and ask (by phone or email) whether they have internship or co-op opportunities for college students. If they do, find out how you can learn more about them.

3. Once you've decided which internship(s)/co-op(s) you'd like to pursue, use your current resumé and an accompanying cover letter to apply for that internship(s)/co-op(s). (Note: If you need help with either your resumé or your cover letter, *get it*—preferably from a counselor at your school's career center. There's absolutely no reason for you to try to create/revise these key documents completely on your own, especially when expertise is available—for free—at your campus career center!)

4. If/when you get an interview for an internship/co-op, be sure to prepare for it thoroughly by working with a campus career counselor to research the organization, practice responding to interview questions (in a *mock interview*—see p. 107 of Sophomore Year), and develop a list of questions you'd like to ask during the interview.

5. If/when you land an internship or a co-op, show the organization you're an outstanding hire by:

- Listening well and asking questions from the get-go.
- Showing up on time and looking professional every day.
- Completing your assigned tasks before deadline.
- Demonstrating your willingness to take on the "grunt" work along with the more-challenging assignments.

You're being evaluated from Day One of your experience—and not just on your technical skills but also on your people skills (e.g., attitude, teamwork, self-motivation). Make a good impression and there's a decent chance you'll eventually be offered a full-time, permanent job with this organization!

• ROAD MAP QUESTIONS •

Passions: Do you enjoy working in your internship/co-op setting? Why or why not? Is your internship/co-op exposing you to *new* interests—ones you didn't know you had before?

_____

_____

_____

_____

Innate talents: Are you good at what you do in your internship? How do you know? Do you have the *hard* skills as well as the *soft* skills (e.g., working well with others, making sound decisions, being self-motivated) you need? If not, how could you develop them?

_____

_____

_____

_____

What matters most: Now that you've seen this setting/career/industry firsthand, does it seem like it will allow you to live the life you want to live after graduation (whatever that may entail!)? If not, what's missing?

_____

_____

_____

_____

The Importance of Volunteer Activities

Participate in additional volunteer activities (see p. 32 of Freshman Year) to further strengthen the key *soft skills* future employers will demand (e.g., communication, teamwork, leadership, initiative)—and to show prospective employers that you actively care about the world around you.

Why

Some core skills are critical to your professional success no matter which field/industry you eventually pursue. Each year, the National Association of Colleges and Employers (an industry trade association for college/university career services professionals and employers who hire new college graduates) asks its employer members which *soft skills* are most important for college students and recent graduates to have. Consistently in the top ten (see p. 29 of Freshman Year) are communication (written and verbal), teamwork, leadership, and initiative (self-motivation).

You not only need to *have* these essential skills by the time you graduate; you also need to be able to *prove* it to prospective employers. As was the case when you did it during your first two years of college, volunteering will allow you to do just that.

But volunteering is more than simply a way for you to develop yourself professionally. Indeed, it goes far beyond *you*. By volunteering, you show future employers (and the rest of the people in your life) that the many needs of the world matter to you, and that you're willing to do something about them in a tangible way. If you were an employer, wouldn't *you* be impressed by an entry-level job candidate who clearly and actively does something about problems he/she sees—without expecting anything in return? That's what volunteering is all about.

How

1. See if your campus has an office devoted to matching students with local volunteer opportunities. (Note: The office will probably be called something like the Office of Volunteer Opportunities or the Service-Learning Office—or it may be a department of a larger organization like the Office of Student/Campus Activities.) If it does, visit the office and learn how you can volunteer in a way that matches your interests and skills and fits into your schedule.

2. If you're involved in a campus organization, see if it coordinates any volunteer activities in your area. If it does, participate. If it doesn't, why not be the person to launch such an effort? (Talk about developing your leadership skills!)

3. Do any of your academic courses include a required *service-learning* component? If so, you've got a built-in volunteer/service experience set up already. If not, why not schedule a course—next semester!—that does have a service-learning component?

4. If you live in a fairly large city, contact its local chapter of the United Way. Often, the United Way serves as the local clearinghouse for volunteer opportunities. Alternatively, use the United Way web site (www.unitedway.org) to search for volunteer opportunities in your area, or use another web-based search tool like VolunteerMatch (www.volunteermatch.org).

5. Once you find a volunteer opportunity to pursue, keep a journal or diary of your activities. What sorts of things are you doing when you volunteer? What are you learning? Write it all down now ... so that you don't forget it later!

• ROAD MAP QUESTIONS •

Passions: What's most interesting about your volunteer activities? Are there any activities you *don't* like? What are they, and why don't you like them?

_____

_____

_____

_____

Innate talents: What new skills are you learning through your volunteer activities? What skills are you developing further? Which of your volunteer activities come ridiculously easy to you? Which ones are quite difficult?

_____

_____

_____

_____

What matters most: Which of your volunteer activities are naturally motivating to you? Why do these activities inspire you so strongly? Conversely, which activities feel forced or uninspiring to you? Why?

_____

_____

_____

_____

dreams ... discoveries ... reflections ...
intentions ... discussions

Mapping Your Direction

Uncovering Your Purpose
Junior Year

"To accomplish great things, we must not only act
but dream, not only plan but also believe."

~ ANATOLE FRANCE

This is the year when you'll need to choose your experiences wisely and perhaps take a few calculated risks as well. Go after your dreams and grab the experiences that fit you best.

Purpose

What has been revealed to you in the activities you've pursued this past year? When have you felt really satisfied in the past few months? Why? What are you now looking forward to, and why does this vision excite you so much?

_____

_____

_____

_____

_____

_____

_____

_____

_____

_____

_____

_____

_____

_____

_____

_____

Dreams—Life's Destinations

Now that you've been exposed to a variety of work and volunteer activities, your natural inclinations will provide a sort of direction through the ebb and flow of your interests. Some of your activities this past year—work, volunteering, service—have no doubt prompted feelings of heightened interest. Which activities did that? How do these connections relate to your dreams? Where do you want to go at this point in your life?

Discoveries

Scenic highways: How connected have you felt to your purpose this year through your various activities—working or interning, volunteering, participating in a student or professional organization? What's become clearer to you with respect to the kind of work you truly love?

_____

_____

_____

_____

_____

_____

Roadblocks and speed bumps: As you think about your experiences of this past year, which ones just didn't resonate with you? Which of them felt awkward ... or just didn't fit your style ... or didn't hold any interest or meaning for you? How might these insights impact your decisions about the work you want to do in life? And what career-related activities would you like to do that you haven't had the time and/or energy for (yet!)?

_____

_____

_____

_____

_____

_____

Reflections

Have you discovered your own wisdom? Set aside some time when you can be completely alone and find a quiet place where you can do some self-reflection. Think about your conduct in relation to other people in your life, and consider what you've both received from and given to these various relationships. What are you grateful for and what do you feel best about? What's important to you in your relationships as you ponder your future career decisions?

In the book *The Myth of Maturity* (W.W. Norton & Company, 2001), author Terri Apter notes that a constant source of disappointment among recent college graduates is the often less-than-satisfying quality of their various workplace relationships. Knowing what a satisfying relationship is for *you* will be critical to you in the coming months as you finish college and head for the world of work.

Intentions

Set your course: What skills or special knowledge do you want to develop this year through your various activities and experiences? What will you commit to that will move you toward gaining this skill/knowledge? What have you observed about your own thoughts and feelings this year as they relate to your work and volunteer experiences? What have you noticed that you want to capitalize on or change?

_____

_____

_____

_____

_____

_____

Daily intentions: How well are you developing relationships in your work settings? Are you satisfied with them? What's important to you in a work relationship? What can you do each time you go to work to make your relationships there more fulfilling?

_____

_____

_____

_____

_____

_____

_____

Discussion and Dialogue

Tapping your support system: What do you want to accomplish this year in your work or internship/co-op experiences? Talk to people in your work/internship/co-op setting and let them know what you'd like to achieve. Then ask each of them if they'd be willing to guide you as you pursue these goals.

Mapping Your Direction

How have your senses, thoughts, feelings, and intuition influenced your decisions this year? Do you have more clarity? What's still confusing to you? How would you evaluate your self-confidence at this point? What do you need to do now to get where you want to be later where your future career is concerned?

_____

_____

_____

_____

_____

_____

_____

_____

_____

_____

_____

_____

_____

_____

_____

_____

_____

Senior Year

• SENIOR YEAR •

Employment and Education

Introduction

Your senior year will probably be the most challenging of your college career. But you've developed many skills over the last three years that will help you exceed your expectations!

There will be times this year when you'll feel overwhelmed because you'll need to:

- Pay attention to your academics so that you keep your grades up.
- Continue picking up solid experience through a job, an internship, or a co-op.
- Take on a leadership role in a campus organization or other group.

You'll also have to focus on the future. So you'll feel like you're living in two worlds at times—college and post-college. Unfortunately, that's just the way it is during your senior year.

But there's good news too: Over the last three years, you've pursued opportunities and wrestled with questions that have likely helped you start seeing the future with a bit more clarity. If not ... go back through your college memories and think about the experiences that have been most meaningful to you. Take the time to ask yourself why. The questions throughout this book are designed to help you better understand your future—your passions, your innate talents, and what matters most to you. It's never too late for you to work through those questions!

The phases of Exploration, Examination, and Experience are behind you. Now it's time to look to the post-graduation future. Whether that means Employment or graduate/professional Education in your particular case, uncovering your purpose is the key to your success and satisfaction.

Academic Activities

• CONTINUING TASKS •

- Continue striving for a cumulative GPA of at least 3.0 (on a 4.0 scale). Continue working particularly hard in your major courses to earn as many A's as you possibly can—B's at a minimum. And if graduate/professional school is in your future, work for an even higher GPA ... as close to 4.0 as possible.

- Continue meeting with your academic advisor at least twice each semester. When you do, be sure you're taking the courses you're supposed to be taking to complete your degree. Take the time to be certain you're meeting all requirements!

- If you plan to study abroad during this, your senior, year (see p. 22 of Sophomore Year), be sure you're still meeting all the academic requirements to graduate on time. Get prior approval for all of your study abroad courses so that you're not surprised—unpleasantly—when you return to campus expecting to graduate.

- Continue taking skills-based courses with your remaining electives— ones that complement your major and ones that are seemingly unrelated to your major. Focus in particular on the areas of computer applications, foreign languages, communication (written and verbal), and research strategies (see p. 125 of Junior Year).

- If you haven't done so already, take a research course or an independent study that allows you to complete a major research project (i.e., a *thesis*) on a topic of strong interest (see p. 131 of Junior Year).

• N E W   T A S K S •

Writing Courses

Strengthen your writing skills by taking an additional writing course or by working on the writing you're doing in other courses.

Why

Depending on the coursework you've taken to this point, you may or may not have had someone critically evaluate your writing outside of your first-year composition course. The papers you've written have certainly been graded for content, but ideally you should have been required to rewrite them at least once to improve your skills.

Strong writing skills separate you from your peers. Remember: Communication (written and verbal) is the No. 1 *soft skill* employers seek in new college graduates, according to annual surveys of employers conducted by the National Association of Colleges and Employers (see p. 29 of Freshman Year).

How

1. Take an additional upper-level writing course that will help you focus specifically on improving your writing (and rewriting and editing!) skills.

2. If your school has a Writing Center (or similarly named office), use it! The staff members there will review your writing and offer helpful feedback on how you can make it better. (Note: Tell the writing advisor you meet with that you're looking for *critical* feedback, and that you want him/her to be tough on you.)

3. Rewrite, rewrite, rewrite. Embrace the process of actually rewriting papers. College is demanding, and sometimes just getting a paper written is the best you can do. But if you work toward finishing your papers

a week early, you'll build in time for other people to critique your writing. You can give your papers to several people—the professor teaching your class, for instance, or a teaching assistant, or a Writing Center advisor, or even a friend who has exceptional writing skills.

• ROAD MAP QUESTIONS •

Passions: Do you enjoy writing? Do you spend extra time on writing assignments just to get the language right?

_____

_____

_____

_____

Innate talents: Are you a strong writer? Are you able to effectively convey your ideas in writing? Does writing come easily to you?

_____

_____

_____

What matters most: Do you value improving your communication skills—especially when it comes to writing? Are you willing to spend extra time on this area if you need to? If so, what will you do to improve your skills?

_____

_____

_____

_____

The Application for Graduation

Complete your application for graduation by the deadline established by your institution.

Why

You do want to graduate ... don't you? Seriously, though, just talk to one student who has missed the application deadline for graduation (and who thus didn't officially graduate until the following semester) and you'll quickly understand how important it is for you to take care of this essential task sooner vs. later.

How

1. Check with your academic advisor or the Registrar's Office at your school to see *exactly* what you need to do (and by when) to officially apply for graduation from your institution.

2. Once you have the paperwork you need to apply for graduation, complete it immediately. Procrastinate on other tasks in your life if you must, but don't put this one off! You don't want to run into any hitches that would prevent you from graduating on time—with your close friends.

3. Once you've submitted your completed application for graduation, *insist* on getting some sort of receipt acknowledging that your application was received and approved. (You'll need this later if your institution somehow claims you never applied for graduation. Yes, it happens ... more often than you might think, unfortunately.)

• ROAD MAP QUESTIONS •

Passions: Are you excited to start putting your knowledge, skills, and experiences to work in the post-college world? Why or why not?

_____

_____

_____

_____

_____

Innate talents: Do you put off little details like applying for graduation, or is it in your nature to get things done right away, without procrastination?

_____

_____

_____

_____

What matters most: Is it important to you to graduate on time, or are you dreading leaving college? Are you spending time planning carefully for the future or are you living in the moment?

_____

_____

_____

_____

_____

Seeking Professional References

Decide which professor you've gotten to know can be the best spokesperson for you, and ask him/her if he/she is willing to be a professional *reference* for you (either for a post-graduation job or for graduate/professional school).

Why

At some point this year, you're going to start applying for post-graduation jobs (or graduate/professional schools, as the case may be). As part of that process, you're going to need some strong *references* who will speak highly of your skills and abilities, your performance, and your commitment to your chosen field.

If you're like most college students, at least one of your best references will come from a professor you've gotten to know very well (and who in turn has gotten to know you very well). If you can get great references from not just one professor but two or three, you'll be even that much more impressive to prospective employers (or graduate/professional school admissions personnel).

How

1. Contact a few of your favorite professors and ask to meet with them. Prepare for these meetings just as you would prepare for other *networking* opportunities. Be ready to ask for what you need—solid references! Bring along your resume, your *leave-behind paper* (see p. 150 of Junior Year) if you have one, and, if applicable, any graduate/professional school application forms the professors might need.

2. Keep in mind that you're probably not the only student asking for a reference from a particular professor. So give the professor all the information he/she might need to do a good job on your reference letter. Ideally your reference letter will be specific and detailed, giving the reader the sense that the writer genuinely knows you and has accurately and thoroughly assessed your abilities, interests, and motivations.

3. If you don't know any of your professors well enough to ask them for a professional reference, it's not too late. Choose a course you're enjoying now and take a moment immediately after an upcoming class session to talk to the professor before he/she leaves the room. Tell him/her that you're finding the course topics genuinely interesting, and that

you'd like to learn more about them outside of class. If you can spend the next few months cultivating a relationship with this professor, he/she just might become a valuable professional reference for you before your college days are over.

• ROAD MAP QUESTIONS •

Passions: Do you feel comfortable sharing what you're passionate about with your professors so that they in turn can act as knowledgeable references for you? Can you communicate your passions clearly, succinctly, and credibly?

_____

_____

Innate talents: Do you have at least one professor who will, for example, write a letter of recommendation for you (for jobs or graduate/professional school), attesting to your skills and abilities in your chosen discipline (or another)?

_____

_____

_____

What matters most: Is there at least one professor who has gotten to know you well enough to understand what truly matters to you in your future career?

_____

_____

_____

Experiential Activities

On-Campus Interviewing

Participate in on-campus interviewing through your school's career center to expose yourself to various companies/organizations and, potentially, land yourself a post-graduation job!

Why

Many employers already have ongoing relationships with career center staff at various colleges/universities—in great part so they can recruit students from those institutions for jobs, internships, and co-op programs.

One of the most common recruiting tools these employers use is *on-campus interviewing* at campus career centers. It's one of the rare times in the world of work when employers are willing to go find—literally and figuratively—prospective job candidates. So you'd be foolish not to take advantage of it.

Typically, campus career centers bring employers to campus in the fall and in the spring. One of those employers might well be looking for *you*. Will they find you? If you participate in on-campus interviewing, you'll certainly improve the odds!

How

1. Contact or stop by your school's career center—or visit its web site— to see when on-campus interviewing will begin in the fall (or in the spring, as the case may be).

2. Complete any registration requirements your career center has in place for participation in on-campus interviewing. (Note: You'll typically have to submit a version of your resumé along with a cover letter. You might also have to complete some demographic information forms.)

3. Prepare for on-campus interviews just as you would any other job interview (see p. 107 in Sophomore Year). Research the organization, dress professionally, and practice responding to questions you think you'll be asked. These are *real interviews* for *real jobs*. So don't try to wing it!

4. Talk to a counselor at the career center and ask him/her to tell you about the organizations you'll be interviewing with during on-campus

recruiting. Campus career counselors almost always have strong working relationships with the employers who come to campus. Why not
tap that expertise?

• ROAD MAP QUESTIONS •

Passions: Are you prepared to share what you're passionate about with
the prospective employers who participate in your campus career center's on-campus interviewing program?

_____

_____

_____

Innate talents: Are you prepared to effectively describe your abilities
and skills to prospective employers? Do you have stories and examples to back up each of your claims? Are those stories and examples
compelling?

_____

_____

_____

What matters most: Are you ready to put interviewing at the top of
your priority list? And will you be able to communicate to prospective
employers what matters most to you in your career and in the organization you work for?

_____

_____

_____

Job-Search Workshops

Attend one or more brief job-search workshops offered by your school's career center.

Why

There's no sense in you tackling your post-graduation job search all by yourself when help is readily available right on campus—in the form of the counselors at your school's career center.

Most career centers offer a variety of short (a few hours or less) seminars and workshops on job-search strategies. Take advantage of them! You'll learn about everything from writing effective resumés and researching organizations to preparing for interviews and negotiating job offers.

How

1. Contact or stop by your school's career center—or visit its web site— to learn about the job-search seminars and workshops it offers. Sign up for the workshop you need the most and gauge how helpful it ends up being for you. If you have a good experience, sign up for other workshops as well.

2. Actively participate in the workshops you attend so that you get the most you can from the experiences.

3. If you have any nagging questions or concerns after a particular workshop, discuss them with the instructor afterwards—either immediately following the workshop or in a one-on-one career counseling appointment a few days later. Don't let your questions go unasked (and thus unanswered)!

• ROAD MAP QUESTIONS •

Passions: How are your deepest passions starting to show themselves in the seminars/workshops you're attending at the campus career center?

_____

_____

_____

_____

Innate talents: How will you effectively describe your innate talents on a resumé, in an interview, or during the networking process? What tips are you picking up from the career center workshops/seminars you're attending?

_____

_____

_____

_____

What matters most: Are the seminars/workshops you're going to helping you clarify what matters most to you in your future career? Why or why not? What types of questions do you have about your work-related values, and how can you start getting some answers to them?

_____

_____

_____

_____

The Job Search Support Group

Get a few of your friends together and create a job search support group.

Why

Your friends can be among your best resources—and sources of support—during this sometimes difficult phase of your life. In some ways, your friends might know you better than you know yourself. So they can often help you process the many decisions you'll be faced with during the job search process.

Sometimes conversations with your friends are the "aha" moments you'll never forget—for example, the night you really figured out what you wanted to do with your life. Friends can also point out your strengths, your innate talents, and your strongest values—all of which factor greatly into your future career.

So invite your friends to participate in an informal job search support group. Help each other help yourselves.

How

1. Ask your friends if they, like you, are stressing out over their post-graduation job searches. You'll likely be surprised at the widespread level of anxiety among your fellow students. Indeed, they may feel relieved that someone else has acknowledged needing support—and taken the lead in making it happen.

2. Meet with the members of your group at least every other week so that you can update each other on your progress (or lack thereof). Ask the other group members to hold you accountable for the tasks you really need to accomplish.

3. If you want to, attend on- and off-campus job/career fairs together. Don't talk to prospective employers as a team or a pack, obviously, but do check in with each other from time to time to share experiences and tips.

• ROAD MAP QUESTIONS •

Passions: What do your friends think you're passionate about? Are they right? Do they see how you can use your passions in a future career—even if you cannot?

_____

_____

_____

_____

Innate talents: What do your friends see as your innate talents? Do you agree? Why or why not?

_____

_____

_____

_____

What matters most: When you ask your friends to identify your top values, do they list the values you see as your most cherished ones? If not, is it possible that your actions sometimes conflict with what really matters to you, especially in a future career?

_____

_____

_____

_____

Evaluating Campus Organization Experience

Evaluate what you've *done* in the campus organizations you're in and prioritize what you still need to *do* during your senior year.

Why

It's one thing to merely participate in a campus organization. But employers who hire new college graduates consistently report that they're looking for grads with *leadership* skills and experience (see p. 29 of Freshman Year). Employers demand specific examples of what you've *accomplished* in college.

Overseeing a student group is a great way for you to build your list of accomplishments and develop sound leadership skills. Now is the time for you to figure out what accomplishments and skills you've already taken care of and, perhaps more importantly, which ones you still need to take care of during this last year of participating in your student group.

How

1. Take a couple of sheets of paper and label them "What I've Done" and "What I Still Need to Do," respectively. Find a quiet place and spend a half-hour or so listing items on each of the sheets. What seems to be taken care of where your leadership skills and accomplishments are concerned? What do you still need to do? Write it all down!

2. Talk to other members of the organization as well as your faculty advisor (if your group has one). What do *they* see as the leadership skills you've already developed and the accomplishments you've already taken care of? And what do *they* think you still need to work on where leadership skills and accomplishments are concerned?

3. Write down a few goals—some commitments about what you'll pursue in the coming months and how. Research has shown time and again that written goals are much more likely than unwritten goals to become *achieved* goals!

4. Follow through on your commitments and remember to write down your challenges and successes as you go—because it will serve as great material for those job interviews you'll soon have!

• ROAD MAP QUESTIONS •

Passions: Is there anything you're passionate about improving in your campus organization? What kind of project or position really motivates you? Why?

_____

_____

_____

_____

Innate talents: What natural abilities and skills do you have that your campus organization could really use? How do you know? How can you use these strengths to make the organization stronger?

_____

_____

_____

What matters most: Are your campus organization's activities genuinely important to you? Why or why not?

_____

_____

_____

_____

Internships and Co-op Experiences

If possible, complete another internship or co-op experience (or your first one if you haven't done one before).

Why

As we've noted throughout this book (see p. 93 of Sophomore Year and p. 164 of Junior Year), today's employers expect you to come out of college with at least *some* hands-on experience in your chosen field. The more of that experience you can accumulate through internships and co-ops, the better.

It's easy to have *too little* career-related experience when you graduate; it's impossible to have *too much*.

How

Here are several ways you can learn about internship and co-op possibilities to pursue:

- Visit your school's career center (or its web site) and check out the internship and co-op listings it has obtained from specific organizations.

- Check out a college-oriented career web site like MonsterTRAK (www.monstertrak.com), Experience (www.experience.com), College Grad (www.collegegrad.com), or CollegeRecruiter (www.collegerecruiter.com) and look for internship and co-op listings there.

- Go to your campus library or a nearby bookstore and look through one of the many printed internship/co-op directories that are on the market (published by companies like Princeton Review and Peterson's). (Note: At the bookstore, you'll find such guides in the "Careers" and/or "College Guides" section.)

- Talk to your professors and fellow students and ask them where current and previous students from your school/department have done internships or co-ops in the past.

- Talk to a counselor at your school's career center (particularly if the center has an *internship coordinator* or similarly titled person on staff). Ask him/her where previous students from your school have interned or done co-ops in the past.

- Directly approach any organizations that interest you and ask (by phone or email) whether they have internship or co-op opportunities for college students. If they do, see how you can find out more about them.

• ROAD MAP QUESTIONS •

Passions: If you're doing another internship in the same field you interned in before, are you continuing to enjoy the industry and the work within that industry? Is your additional internship/co-op experience *affirming* your choice of field/industry?

_____

_____

_____

_____

_____

Innate talents: Have you discovered that you're good at the work involved in this field/industry? Does your additional internship/co-op experience tell you anything new about your abilities and skills in relation to the field/industry—i.e., will you be successful in it?

_____

_____

_____

_____

_____

_____

What matters most: Does the additional internship/co-op experience you're obtaining tell you anything more about what working in this field/industry means to you? Will this line of work give you the type of life you want? Is it going to allow you to pursue whatever it is that's most important to you (e.g., achieving financial wealth, making a difference to society, tapping your creativity and independence)?

_____

_____

_____

_____

_____

_____

_____

_____

The Graduation Ceremony

Attend your graduation ceremony.

Why

Some college students decide not to participate in their school's graduation ceremony. But you really do miss out on a once-in-a-lifetime experience if you choose not to attend your own graduation. You deserve to pick up that beautiful diploma you've been working so hard to obtain—and to be recognized, publicly, for your efforts!

How

1. At most schools, you have to officially apply for graduation (see p. 185 of Senior Year)—typically several weeks or even a few months before your expected graduation date. Check with your academic advisor or the Registrar's Office to see exactly what you need to do, and when, to participate in your graduation ceremony.

2. Be sure to order your cap and gown on time from your campus bookstore (or whatever campus department handles caps and gowns).

3. If you want to, order some printed invitations that you can send out to family and friends who may want to attend your graduation. Be sure you understand and observe the ordering deadlines established by your campus bookstore (or whatever campus department handles graduation invitations).

4. Go to your ceremony, have fun, listen to what the speaker has to say, take tons of pictures, and celebrate mightily afterwards. Congratulations! You've made it!

• ROAD MAP QUESTIONS •

Passions: Have you really explored your passions during college? What would you do differently if you could?

_____

_____

_____

Innate talents: Has the education you've received strengthened your innate talents? What experiences have you benefited the most from over the past four years? What have those experiences given you where your future career is concerned—especially when it comes to new skills and expertise?

_____

_____

_____

_____

What matters most: Has your college experience helped you solidify what you want for your future—especially with respect to your career plans? What *do* you want, and why?

_____

_____

_____

_____

Focus on the Future

• CONTINUING TASKS •

- Continue developing your career portfolio, and update it continuously (see p. 144 of Junior Year).

- Continue researching careers in depth by not only reading about them, but also talking (in person or via phone/email) with people who actually work in them (*informational interviewing*—see p. 97 of Sophomore Year). Boost your efforts by asking a campus reference librarian to show you how to obtain hard(er)-to-find information on companies/organizations that interest you. Make it your goal to "out-research" your fellow students (i.e., your competition).

- Continue attending job/career fairs—on and off campus. Go to as many as you can (see p. 214 of Senior Year).

• NEW TASKS •

The Basic Cover Letter

Write a basic cover letter that you'll be able to send to prospective employers (or graduate/professional schools, as the case may be).

Why

You can't send out a resumé without an accompanying cover letter. Period. Prospective employers will look to your cover letter to:

- Learn about your very best traits, abilities, and achievements.
- Get an initial sense of your written communication skills.

They'll also look for evidence that you've researched *their* particular organization and *their* particular job opening. Like all of us, employers have egos: They want you to apply not just for any job in any organization, but *their* job in *their* organization.

How

1. Start a new document in Microsoft Word (the most widely used word processing program, by far) and save it as "Basic Cover Letter." It's smart to include the date as part of the file name—e.g., "John Smith—Basic Cover Letter—10December2006."

2. On the top left-hand side of the page, type your name and contact information (including address, phone number, and email address). This will obviously take several lines.

3. Next, hit the "Enter" key on your computer a couple of times to leave a little white space. Then type today's date.

4. Now, leave a little white space again and type the name and address of the person you're writing to.

5. Next, it's time to begin your actual letter. Whenever possible, address your letter to a specific person—e.g., "Dear Ms. Johnson" or "Dear Dr. Evans." But if you can't track down a specific name, use a generic phrase like "Dear Hiring Manager" or "Dear Recruiter."

6. Your letter itself will be made up of three to five short paragraphs:

- In the first paragraph, describe why you're writing and how you learned of the position you're applying for. Try to work in a brief mention of one or two of your key skills as well.

- In the second and third paragraphs, highlight any key traits, abilities and skills, or achievements you have that you believe the letter recipient will want to know about. (This is the place where you outline the very best you have to offer.)

- In the fourth paragraph, ask to meet with the letter recipient to discuss the position in more detail (i.e., an interview). Stress the various ways the recipient can get in touch with you.

- In the final paragraph, thank the recipient for his/her time.

- End with "Sincerely"—followed by three or four blank lines— then your name. (If you'll be sending your letter in print form, be sure to sign it first!)

7. Once you have a first-draft cover letter completed, set up an appointment with a counselor at your school's career center. Let him/her know in advance that you'd like to use your meeting to evaluate your cover letter.

8. At your meeting with the counselor, take detailed notes on suggested changes and make them accordingly afterwards.

9. Keep in mind that your cover letter will change slightly with each job (or school) you apply to. Customize it each time you use it! "One size fits all" usually fits none.

10. Watch for errors when you're customizing your letter. Proofread the letter each and every time you send it to an employer. It's too easy to overlook routine changes such as the recipient's name, title, company, and address.

• ROAD MAP QUESTIONS •

Passions: Does your excitement for this position—and your chosen field—come across in your cover letter? Will your letter set you apart from other candidates?

_____

_____

_____

_____

Innate talents: Do you have the writing skills necessary to land the job (or admission to the graduate/professional school program) you're trying to pursue? Is your cover letter doing you justice?

_____

_____

_____

_____

What matters most: Does your cover letter illustrate that you'll be a good fit for the organization and its customers/clients? Do your values match those of the organization?

_____

_____

_____

_____

_____

Revising the Resumé

Revise your resumé to reflect the experiences, skills, and accomplishments you gained during junior year and the summer following junior year.

Why

As you know by now, a resumé is a living document that needs to change as you grow professionally. It would be foolish for you to write your resumé once and then rest on it. After all, as you progress through your college years, you gain more and more experiences, skills, and accomplishments to brag about!

How

1. Make an appointment with a counselor at your school's career center and let him/her know that you'd like to spend your time together revising your resumé.

2. Before your appointment, take three sheets of paper—as you've done in years past—and label them "New Experiences," "New Skills," and "New Accomplishments," respectively.

3. Take your "New Experiences" sheet and start jotting down any new experiences you can think of that have occurred between your junior year and now. *Do not limit yourself at this point!* If something jumps into your mind—no matter how minor or insignificant it might seem— write it down! The idea is to do a "brain dump" and get everything out of your head and onto paper. Later, you and your career counselor can decide what to add to your resumé and what to leave off.

4. Go through the same "brain dump" exercise with your "New Skills" and "New Accomplishments" sheets. Again, *do not limit yourself at this point!*

5. Once you've finished writing down everything you can think of on each of these sheets, keep them in a handy spot … just in case you think of other entries to add later.

6. Bring the sheets to your appointment with the career counselor and tell him/her you've written down everything you can think of. Ask him/her to help you remember anything you may have forgotten or disregarded.

7. With the counselor's help, decide which entries to add to your resumé and which to leave off. As usual, you'll almost certainly have to do some reformatting of your resumé to accommodate the changes.

8. Once you've finished revising your resumé, ask your counselor to look at it one last time for minor revisions.

• ROAD MAP QUESTIONS •

Passions: Do the activities listed on your resumé effectively illustrate your interests and passions?

_____

_____

_____

Innate talents: Will employers (or graduate/professional schools, as the case may be) be able to easily spot your top abilities and skills on your resumé? And will they see your _achievements_, not just your _activities/duties_?

_____

_____

_____

What matters most: Does your finished resumé accurately represent you? Will it be your ticket into an interview for a position that is truly important to you?

_____

_____

_____

Get a Second Opinion

Work closely with a campus career counselor and other experts (e.g., a knowledgeable professor, your internship and/or job supervisors and colleagues) to assess—and, if necessary, improve—the *strength* of your resumé and the *strength* of your cover letter.

Why

If, all by yourself, you write the strongest resumé and the strongest cover letter possible—on the very first try—then you're a one-in-a-million case! In reality, none of us can develop a truly solid resumé or cover letter without a few additional sets of eyes—i.e., constructive feedback from other people.

If you really want your resumé and cover letter to be the best they can be, you'll readily acknowledge—and welcome—the ongoing suggestions you receive from knowledgeable people you can trust.

How

1. Once you have a resumé and cover letter *you're* happy with, start showing the documents to other people. For example, if you haven't been working with a career counselor at your school's career center, now is the time to see one so you can get some expert feedback on your documents. Remember: You're shooting for not merely *adequate* documents but *outstanding* ones!

2. Ask others to critique your documents as well—favorite professors, internship or job supervisors and co-workers, members of any professional groups you're in, and your parents (or friends/colleagues of your parents).

3. Carefully note the feedback you receive from each person. Keep in mind, however, that these documents are *yours!* You have final decision-making power over what feedback to use and what feedback to ignore. If you get a suggestion that seems to make sense, use it. But if you get a suggestion that doesn't seem to make sense, let it go.

4. Use the feedback you receive (the feedback that seems good to you, that is!) to polish your resumé and cover letter one more time before you start sending them out. Know, however, that you'll never truly be done with the revision process. Resumés and cover letters are living documents that change with both your career development and the circumstances you're tackling.

• ROAD MAP QUESTIONS •

Passions: Do your final resumé and cover letter accurately reflect what you're most passionate about?

_____

_____

_____

_____

Innate talents: Will employers (or graduate/professional schools, as the case may be) be able to easily spot your top abilities and skills on your final resumé? And will they see your _achievements_, not just your _activities/duties_?

_____

_____

_____

_____

What matters most: Do the experiences you've highlighted on your final resumé and in your final cover letter reflect your values? Will employers view those values positively or negatively?

_____

_____

_____

_____

Highlighting Abilities, Traits, and Accomplishments for Interviewing

Start jotting down stories from your past experiences that you can use in interviews to highlight your abilities, skills, traits, and achievements.

Why

Employers are savvy and skeptical. They've heard entry-level job applicants say things like "I have strong communication skills" and "I'm a good team player" hundreds of times. They've also been burned (often more than once) by job applicants who have made such claims in their interviews but demonstrated just the opposite once on the job.

In your interviews, you have to be ready to back up what you say about your abilities, skills, traits, and achievements. You can do that with brief stories from your past—from internships, classroom experiences, volunteering, and elsewhere—that serve as *evidence* of the abilities, skills, traits, and achievements you're claiming.

How

1. While you never know exactly what employers are going to ask you about in job interviews, you can easily make some educated guesses. Either on your own or, better yet, with the help of a counselor at your school's career center, write down the abilities, skills, traits, and achievements that the employers in *your* chosen field will most likely seek in any candidate for an entry-level job in the field. If, for example, you plan to go into accounting, you can be sure that a prospective employer is going to wonder about your ability to crunch complex numbers. If you want to go into social work, a prospective employer is no doubt going to ask you about your helping skills and experiences.

2. For each ability, skill, trait, or achievement you write on your list, think about one specific example from your previous experience that will show an employer you indeed possess that ability, skill, trait, or achievement. Use the following STAR acronym to write your stories down in detail:

   - ST = Situation you had to deal with, or Task you had to perform
   - A = Action
   - R = Result

Suppose, for example, you anticipate that prospective employers are going to ask about your problem-solving skills. Here are some brief notes on a story you could tell to demonstrate your problem-solving abilities:

- ST = I was working with a group in my 400-level psych class and one of the people in my group wasn't pulling his weight on the major project we had to complete.

- A = I met him for lunch and asked him if there was something going on in his life that was preventing him from being more helpful to our group. Turns out his father was in the hospital and he was very distracted. So, with his permission, I went to the rest of the group and asked if each of them (me included) would be willing to take a small piece of his responsibilities so he could take an incomplete for the course and spend more time with his father.

- R = The group members quickly agreed to each take a part of the student's duties, and we were able to move forward—without him losing face.

3. Keep the notes about your stories in a file on your computer so that you can continually add to them. (This is not the time to scribble things down on pieces of scrap paper—and then lose them!)

• ROAD MAP QUESTIONS •

Passions: Do your stories illustrate what you're passionate about? How do you know you're being compelling?

_____

_____

_____

_____

Innate talents: Do your stories reflect your strongest abilities and skills?

_____

_____

_____

_____

What matters most: Will your stories help you answer interview questions in a way that will illustrate what's important to you?

_____

_____

_____

_____

Looking for Post-Graduation Job Opportunities

Start looking for post-graduation job opportunities.

Why

Now is the time to start your post-graduation job search in earnest. It typically takes at least a few months to find an entry-level job, and it can take longer if the economy and the job market are sluggish.

How

Here are ten specific ways you can look for entry-level job possibilities:

1. Visit your school's career center. Take advantage of the services available to you right on campus—if for no other reason than the fact that your tuition and fee dollars are helping to pay for them!

2. Network (see p. 148 of Junior Year). Talk to people to either track down helpful contacts or learn about job openings that may not necessarily be widely advertised (if they're advertised at all). Start by talking to your own family, friends, and acquaintances. Let everyone in your life know that you're looking for a job, and give them an idea of what type of job it is.

3. Contact professional associations in your field (see p. 156 of Junior Year). National, regional, and local professional groups exist in great part to help their members with their career development. As such, many organizations include field-specific job listings on their web sites or in their printed publications.

4. Visit company/organization web sites. Many companies and organizations post their job openings right on their own web sites (usually under an "Employment" or "Career Opportunities" or similarly titled section).

5. Apply directly to companies/organizations that interest you. Do you want to work specifically for Company X or Organization Y? If so, send a well-written cover letter and your resumé directly to the company, either to its *human resources* office or, often more effective, to the person who would likely make hiring decisions for the part of the organization that interests you.

6. Attend job/career fairs (see p. 214). Many cities—particularly large ones—host job/career fairs, at various locations, throughout the year. Most colleges and universities hold their own job/career fairs as well, either individually or in collaboration with other institutions. A job/career fair is one of the few opportunities you'll ever have for employers *to come to you.*

7. Use college-specific web sites like MonsterTRAK (www.monster trak.com), Experience (www.experience.com), CollegeRecruiter (www.collegerecruiter.com), and College Grad (www.collegegrad.com). These sites and others feature job listings geared specifically to college students and recent graduates. In most cases, you can also upload your resumé into the databases the sites offer to prospective employers.

8. Use general web sites like Monster (www.monster.com), CareerBuilder (www.careerbuilder.com), and HotJobs (www.hotjobs.com) as well as niche sites targeting your particular field. These sites feature job listings geared toward a more diverse group of job seekers. And, like their college-specific counterparts, most allow you to upload your resumé.

9. Use a placement agency. There are companies out there that specialize in helping people find jobs. Some of them even focus on working with college students and recent graduates. Maybe one of them can help you. A word of caution, however: While most of these organizations receive their fees from *employers* (and not *you*, the job seeker), some will seek money from you. Avoid the ones that charge *you*.

10. Consider temping. Often, by working as a *temp* (i.e., temporary employee) for a company for a short length of time, you can position yourself to be hired for a full-time, permanent position that opens up later on in the organization. Even if that doesn't happen, though, temping will help you see various companies from the inside, meet people in your field of interest, and earn some decent money in most cases.

• ROAD MAP QUESTIONS •

Passions: Now that you're a senior—with much more knowledge, experience, and expertise than you had as a freshman—what settings/careers/industries appeal to you the most? What types of jobs do you want to try for? Why?

Innate talents: In what settings/careers/industries will you most likely perform the best?

_____

_____

_____

_____

_____

What matters most: Which settings/careers/industries will most likely allow you to live the kind of life you want to live?

_____

_____

_____

_____

Job/Career Fairs

Attend job/career fairs—on and off campus—to talk to prospective employers so that you can try to land job interviews.

Why

Going to a job/career fair is the most efficient and effective way for you to meet a whole bunch of employers at the same time—employers who are in hiring mode to boot! (Why else would they participate in a job/career fair, after all?) It's a comparatively rare opportunity for you to make many professional connections—in a very short period of time—with people who are ready to talk to you.

How

1. Stop by your school's career center (or visit its web site) to see what on- and off-campus job/career fairs are coming up over the next several months. Watch the career section of your local newspaper as well, and contact any local government or nonprofit career agencies in your area to see if they're aware of upcoming job/career fairs.

2. Determine which job/career fairs you'll be attending and put them into your formal schedule or day planner. These are not events you want to forget or blow off!

3. Think of each job/career fair experience in terms of what you should do *before*, *during*, and *after*:

Before

- Make sure your resumé is in solid shape. (If it isn't, ask a campus career counselor to help you improve it—see p. 205.) Print plenty of copies of your resumé when it's done so that you can hand it out to employers at the fair without fear of running out!

- Create some basic business cards. You can buy blank business cards at any office supply store and create your own finished cards in a word processing program. You can then print your cards on a laser printer or inkjet. No need to get super-fancy; simply include your name, contact information, and perhaps your major and/or your broad career goals.

- Research the organizations that will be attending the fair. Visit their web sites to find out what they do. Make sure you're ready when an employer asks, "So, what do you know about us?"

- Spend a few minutes plotting—ahead of time—which employers you want to see at the job/career fair. Write down your top priorities, the next-most-important priorities, and so on. You want to use your time at the fair as efficiently as possible.

- Develop a thirty-second "commercial" about yourself. When an employer invariably says to you, "Tell me about yourself," you need to have something intelligent—and brief—to say to get the conversation going. So develop a thirty-second spiel ahead of time, and practice it with a friend or a campus career counselor so that it comes easily and naturally to you.

During

- When you arrive at the job/career fair—with many copies of your resumé in hand!—check in at the registration table, pick up any materials that are being handed out, and put on a name tag if one is offered to you.

- Pull out your list of top-priority companies/organizations and start visiting their tables. (Note: If you feel the need to warm up a bit, visit one of your lower-priority companies first!)

- Introduce yourself at each table and offer your hand for a handshake. Be sure your handshake is firm but not bone-breaking. (Note: Practice your handshake beforehand if you need to. It might seem silly, but your handshake is an important first impression of you.)

- Dress appropriately. This is not the time for shorts and flip-flops. At a minimum, dress *business casual*—maybe not suit and tie, but certainly looking professional and presentable in nice-looking, cleaned-and-pressed clothes. If in doubt, *overdress*. (Note: It should go without saying that you'll want to be well groomed, too. And you may want to lose the nose ring for the day.)

- Ask good questions. Employers are impressed by job candidates who ask intelligent questions about the company, the job, the work environment, and the broader industry the company serves.

- Talk about what you offer, not what you want. You'll be a refreshing change of pace for the employer if you focus mostly on what you can do *for him/her*—instead of constantly asking about what the employer can do *for you*.

- Leave your resumé and business card with each employer you talk to.

After

- Immediately after the job/career fair, write detailed notes about who you visited with, what you discussed, and what you learned. You *won't* remember it all a week from now, when the names and faces of the various employers start to run together in your mind.

- Follow up on any promises you made. If you told an employer you'd send him/her something, do it. If you said you'd call or email, do it.

If you don't, employers will likely perceive your lack of follow up as lack of caring—and promptly drop you from their A-list.

- Send a thank-you note to each employer you talked to at any length. It's common courtesy and, as importantly, it will make you stand out from the vast majority of other job seekers who don't bother sending thank-you notes.

• ROAD MAP QUESTIONS •

Passions: Which of the companies/organizations at the job/career fair excite you the most, and why? Do they offer any particular products, services, or causes that truly tap your passions? Can you envision yourself having a blast working forty (or more) hours a week for a particular organization? Why?

_____

_____

_____

_____

Innate talents: Which of the companies/organizations would tap your best (and favorite) abilities and skills? What sorts of things could you do for these organizations? Where are your talents truly needed? How might you effectively market your talents to the organizations that could use them the most?

_____

_____

_____

_____

What matters most: Did you learn about any companies/organizations whose products, services, or causes match up with what's most important to you in life? Which of the companies/organizations could you really *believe in* at your core, and why? Conversely, which companies/organizations turned out to be real turnoffs for you, and why? Have you learned anything about what you *don't* want in your job or in the organization you work for?

_____

_____

_____

_____

_____

_____

Identifying Professional References

Identify three or four people who are both willing and able to serve as *professional references* for you.

Why

Practically all prospective employers will want to talk to people—i.e., your *professional references*—who know you well and can speak to your abilities, skills, traits, and experiences.

Sometimes employers will want to contact your references before they bring you in for an interview. Most often, though, they'll want to talk to your references *after* they've interviewed you—when they're almost (but not quite) ready to offer you the job. In either case, you need to have some people lined up who will speak highly of you and assure the employer that hiring you is a wise move.

How

1. Think about people in your life who would be willing and able to serve as positive professional references for you. Consider professors who know you well, advisors and/or counselors, internship/co-op/work supervisors, and others in positions of significant influence.

2. Contact each of the people on your list and ask them if they'd be willing to be a professional reference for you. For each of the people who agree to be a reference, prepare a brief list of the abilities, skills, traits, and accomplishments you hope they'll be able to highlight (on your behalf) when they talk to prospective employers who inquire about you. Help your references help you!

3. Ask each of your references to write you a one- or two-page *letter of recommendation* that you can keep for future reference. While many employers these days will *not* take the time to read these letters, a few might. Either way, *you* will have a written record of the insights each of your references provides on your behalf.

4. Prepare a printed list of your references, with full contact information for each one. If—make that *when!*—an employer asks you for your references, you can then send or email him/her your printed list.

5. Alert each of your references when you have a feeling a particular employer may be contacting them to ask about you. You don't want your reference people to be caught off guard!

• ROAD MAP QUESTIONS •

Passions: Have you told your references what it is you dream about and why you're passionate about it? Do they know your ideal work setting? career? industry? Are you sure?

_____

_____

_____

_____

Innate talents: Have you asked your references what they think you're really good at? Do their assessments match your own? Have you shared with them how you've been developing your innate talents and building your skills?

_____

_____

_____

_____

What matters most: Do your references understand what truly motivates you? Do they know what's most important to you, especially in your future career?

_____

_____

_____

_____

Using the Career Portfolio

Work with a campus career counselor to learn how to use your *career portfolio* effectively in interviews.

Why

Last year, you (hopefully!) created a *career portfolio* (see p. 144 of Junior Year) using the many items you (hopefully!) began saving starting freshman year. (Note: If you didn't create a career portfolio last year, now's the time.)

It's one thing to *have* a career portfolio; it's quite another to know how to *use* your portfolio effectively—especially where it matters most: in interviews. A counselor at your school's career center can help you practice this key skill so that you'll confidently and competently present essential highlights from your portfolio in your interviews—in a way that doesn't overwhelm or, worse, turn off the person you're talking to.

Remember: Your portfolio is intended to help you back up your claims in an interview situation. It's a presentation *tool*; it's not a presentation in and of itself. In other words, you can't simply go into an interview, hand your career portfolio to the employer, and sit back and watch. Instead, you need to learn how to incorporate your portfolio into your overall presentation of yourself. It's a little bit science and a lot of art—but you can learn how to do it effectively if you're simply willing to practice ahead of time.

How

1. Set up a meeting with a counselor at your school's career center. Tell him/her you have a career portfolio and that you'd like to practice using it in an interview situation. (Note: If possible, have your counselor videotape your practice session—much as you'd do for a mock interview [see p. 107 of Sophomore Year]—so you can review your performance together afterward.)

2. With your career counselor's help, work on the following activities as they relate to using your portfolio in an interview:

   • Introducing to the employer the fact that you have a portfolio in the first place.

   • Guiding an employer through your complete portfolio if he/she should ask. (Note: This is comparatively rare; most employers simply don't have the time or the desire to go through your entire portfolio, page by page. But it *does* happen, so you need to be ready for this possibility.)

- Highlighting key pages in your portfolio based on specific questions an employer might ask. Example: "Tell me about a time when you led a team to accomplish something." Possible response: Showing the employer the page in your portfolio featuring a letter you received from the president of your college, congratulating a team you led that raised a record amount of scholarship money for the school.

- Figuring out what to do if the employer wants you to leave your portfolio behind. (Note: Generally, you *don't* want to do this—unless you have a complete backup copy! But you can, for example, leave a mini-portfolio of key documents with the employer, or offer to make copies of key portfolio elements and leave them behind.)

3. Ask your career counselor if there are any parts of your portfolio that could be stronger and, if so, how you can improve them. If/when you make these improvements, practice presenting them to your career counselor in a follow-up session.

4. Set a goal of knowing your portfolio inside and out, backwards and for-wards. Practice with your career counselor until you can quickly turn to any particular page in your portfolio. You don't want to find yourself stumbling and stalling in an interview situation! You'll be far more impressive to the employer when you easily—and confidently—lead him/her through the key elements of your portfolio.

• ROAD MAP QUESTIONS •

Passions: When you present your career portfolio (in whole or in part) to an interviewer, will he/she get a good idea of what your strongest interests are? If not, how can you address this problem?

_____

_____

_____

Innate talents: Does your portfolio offer evidence that you have the abilities and skills you say you have, as well as the ones a particular employer is looking for? Do *you* do a good job of presenting the elements of your portfolio so that your key abilities and skills are crystal clear to the employer?

_____

_____

_____

What matters most: When an employer looks at your portfolio, will he/she be able to easily spot what's important to you, especially where your career is concerned? And will you be able to effectively present these essential career values to the employer, using your portfolio as a visual backdrop?

_____

_____

_____

Interviewing

Interview for as many jobs as you reasonably can.

Why

For most people, interviewing is an odd and unnerving experience. But the more interviewing you do, the better you tend to become at it—and the more comfortable you become with the process.

Just as you didn't learn to ride a bike or play the guitar in a day or two, you won't be outstanding at interviewing after a time or two (or three or four!). But as you go through more interviews, you'll improve. And all the while, you'll increase your chances of landing a job.

How

1. Use the strategies outlined in the "Looking for Post-Graduation Job Opportunities" section (see p. 211) to pursue job leads. If—make that *when!*—an employer invites you to interview for a position, enthusiastically accept.

2. When the employer asks when you're available to interview, tell him/her that you'll adjust your schedule to meet his/her needs. If it means skipping a class, so be it. There are times in life when you have to make a sacrifice for an important cause, and this is definitely one of those times! You want to show the employer that his/her needs are important to you.

3. Once you have an interview set up, be sure to write down the day, time, and location—immediately—in your calendar. You don't want to have to call back later to be reminded of when your interview is (or *was!*).

4. Prepare for the interview by researching the company/organization in considerable depth. You *must* be able to show the employer that you know something about his/her organization. If you can't, the employer will conclude you're not serious about the job or his/her organization.

5. Either on your own or, better yet, with the help of a counselor at your school's career center, start thinking about the abilities, skills, traits, and achievements this employer is most likely to ask you about. Determine which of your STAR stories (see p. 209) you'll tell in response to each question you predict will be asked by your interviewer(s).

6. Practice telling your STAR stories to a friend or, even better, a counselor at your school's career center. Have your friend/counselor ask you the questions you predict to be asked. Tell him/her to phrase the questions in a *behavioral* format that requires you to give examples to back up your claims. For example, instead of asking, "How are your communication skills?" your friend/counselor can say, "Tell me about a time when you had to use good communication skills to solve a difficult problem." (Note: Employers will often use phrases like "Tell me about a time when ..." or "Give me an example of ..." in their questioning. This is a strong signal to you that you need to start telling your STAR stories!)

7. On the day of your interview, arrive a few (five to ten) minutes early. Be friendly and courteous to *everyone* you talk to. If you're offered coffee or water, graciously accept.

8. After your interview is over, thank your interviewer(s) graciously and then—within twenty-four hours—send or email a thank-you note. In the note, genuinely thank the interviewer(s) for his/her/their time, reiterate your interest in the job (assuming you *are* still interested!), and restate your key abilities and traits.

• ROAD MAP QUESTIONS •

Passions: Do your strongest interests align with the work of the organization you're interviewing with? Why or why not?

_____

_____

_____

_____

Innate talents: Will you be able to frequently use your strongest abilities and skills in the position you're interviewing for? Will you struggle in the position or will you be successful in it?

_____

_____

_____

_____

What matters most: Do you believe in the mission and vision of the organization you're interviewing with? Why or why not?

_____

_____

_____

_____

"Plan B"

Develop a "Plan B" outlining what actions you'll take after graduation if you haven't yet landed a job by that time.

Why

It's possible—especially if the economy and the job market are sluggish—that you won't be able to land a job before you graduate from college. Don't panic! It's a frequent occurrence, and it's not a sign of your impending doom!

Your best bet is to create a "Plan B"—actions you'll take to make yourself the best job candidate you can possibly be. What's most important to employers is that you continue building your skills and acquiring new experiences during this time of transition. Employers will be impressed with how you've spent your time if you've been creative, resourceful, and inventive.

How

1. If necessary, look for a pay-the-bills type of job that will allow you to stay afloat financially, yet still give you enough time to search for the post-graduation job you really want.

2. If you've been practicing networking strategies during your college years, now is the time to start re-contacting people you've gotten to know. Don't be afraid—or too proud—to ask for help. Remember: You're not the only college graduate—present or past—who wasn't able to land a job before school was over.

3. To the degree you can, maintain a positive attitude. Try to see this time of your life as a learning opportunity—one you'll probably never forget. The art of finding a job is a valuable skill that you'll use for the rest of your working life. By perfecting it now—by choice or by circumstance—you'll feel more confident during future job transitions.

4. In your post-graduation action plan, commit to daily activities that will keep you moving ahead in securing a job. Among the most important activities: networking, searching for jobs, sending out resumés and cover letters, following up on leads, writing thank-you notes, and conducting informational interviews. A job is not going to find you; you'll have to find the job—and that involves *action*.

• ROAD MAP QUESTIONS •

Passions: What activity could you schedule each day to ensure your attitude stays positive? What do you love to do?

_____

_____

_____

_____

_____

Innate talents: What are some ways you can use—and thus stay connected to—your favorite abilities and skills each day?

_____

_____

_____

_____

What matters most: Are you participating in _something_ that matters deeply to you—even if it's only a volunteer experience—so that you feel like you're still contributing to a cause or an organization that's truly important to you? If not, why not?

_____

_____

_____

_____

Post-Graduate Education

Begin researching graduate/professional schools and programs to see which ones interest you most.

Why

You'll be investing a substantial amount of your time, energy, and money to attend graduate or professional school (if you choose to go). So it's critical for you to find the program that's the right fit for you—one that will help you achieve your career goals. Thorough research will help you do just that.

How

1. Either on your own or with the help of a counselor at your school's career center, start researching graduate/professional schools and programs in your field of interest. Some key resources you can use:

   - Print guides to graduate/professional schools (found in your campus career center or library or in any decent-sized bookstore). These guides are published by companies like Peterson's and Princeton Review.

   - Internet sites like Peterson's (www.petersons.com) and Princeton Review (www.princetonreview.com).

   - The web sites of specific schools and programs you're considering.

2. Collect information from the schools and programs that interest you the most. Identify the ones for which you'll be academically eligible for acceptance by looking at their GPA requirements, their course or major requirements, and their minimum entrance exam scores.

3. Talk to people who have firsthand experience with the programs and schools you're considering. They'll be able to give you a sense of what the program/school is like in the trenches, day to day.

4. As you start to narrow your choices down to two or three schools/programs, contact the chairperson (or another faculty member) of each program's academic department and ask questions. Do the same thing with the graduate school/program admissions counselors for each school/program you're seriously considering.

• ROAD MAP QUESTIONS •

Passions: Do the graduate/professional schools and programs you're considering fit with your true passions? How will obtaining a graduate/professional degree from a particular school or program help you live your passions in a career?

_____

_____

_____

_____

Innate talents: Will the graduate/professional schools and programs you're considering strengthen your natural abilities and teach you essential new skills as well?

_____

_____

_____

_____

What matters most: Once you earn a graduate/professional degree from a particular school/program, will you be able to pursue a career doing things that are really important to you?

_____

_____

_____

_____

Graduate/Professional School Entrance Exams

Take your graduate/professional school entrance exams (e.g., GRE, GMAT, LSAT, MCAT), if applicable to your plans.

Why

You won't get into graduate/professional school without first jumping through the required hoops. The two main hoops are an entrance exam (required by many graduate/professional schools, though not all) and an application of some sort.

Pay attention to the date of the entrance exam. You may want to allow yourself enough time to take the test twice in case your first test scores don't reflect your best work. Remember, too, that it's always possible you'll get sick or run into bad weather the day of your entrance exam. So plan to take your entrance exam sooner versus later.

How

1. If you know you'll be going to graduate/professional school following graduation, start working with your academic advisor and/or a campus career counselor early in your senior year in order to get ready.

2. With your advisor's/counselor's help, figure out which entrance exam(s) (if any) you'll need to take in order to be considered for graduate/professional school.

3. With your advisor's/counselor's help (if necessary), obtain the application materials you'll need to complete so you can sign up to take your graduate/professional school entrance exam(s). (Note: Often, your school's career center or graduate school will have the various graduate/professional school entrance exam applications right on hand. But you can also obtain them directly from the various testing companies themselves, right on their web sites.)

4. Complete the application materials immediately and send them in (with appropriate fees) well before the application deadline highlighted in the materials. A few (or several) weeks later, you'll be notified (by the testing company) about when and where you'll be taking your entrance exam.

5. Consider preparing for your entrance exam by purchasing a self-study workbook from your local bookstore or taking one of the many preparation classes offered by the various testing companies.

6. If you haven't done so already, tell the companies that administered your graduate/professional school entrance exam(s) where to send your results (i.e., the schools/programs you've applied to).

• ROAD MAP QUESTIONS •

Passions: Which parts of your entrance exam are you most excited about preparing for? Does your anticipation seem congruent with the topics you enjoyed studying during your undergraduate years? How can you use this clue as you explore graduate/professional programs and schools?

_____

_____

_____

_____

Innate talents: As you prepare for your entrance exam(s), are you identifying which areas are your strongest? How? How will this knowledge help you the day of the exam? Conversely, which areas of the exam should you prepare for more diligently?

_____

_____

_____

_____

_____

What matters most: Have you made it a priority to prepare for your graduate/professional school entrance exam(s), or have you left it to the last minute—or, worse, decided you won't prepare at all? What do these actions (or lack thereof) reveal about your feelings where attending graduate/professional school is concerned?

_____

_____

_____

_____

_____

Applying for Graduate/Professional School

Complete and send in your graduate/professional school application well before the deadline specified by the school/program you're applying to.

Why

One of the easiest (and most common) ways to take yourself out of the running for the graduate/professional school program you're applying to is to miss the application deadline. So send your application(s) in early!

Many graduate/professional school applications are due in late November or early December. So you need to plan ahead to ensure you submit all the pieces of your application(s) on time. You'll likely need the following items, at a minimum:

- The graduate/professional school application itself.
- Your graduate/professional school entrance exam scores.
- Reference letters.
- A personal statement.
- Academic transcripts.
- Evidence of certain experience (depending on the program/school).

If you're applying to a physical therapy program, for instance, it may require you to have a certain number of volunteer hours in a related area. A very specialized program may require experience that is unique to the field you're trying to get into.

How

1. Get applications from the graduate/professional schools and programs you'd like to pursue. (Note: These days, you can usually get them on an institution's web site, but on occasion you may have to call/email and have them sent to you.)

2. Fill out your application materials carefully, completely, and neatly.

3. If you need to prepare an application essay or *personal statement* (see p. 236) of some sort, work closely with your academic advisor and/or a counselor at your school's career center to write a draft, revise, write another draft, revise again, and write your final draft for submission.

4. Send in your completed application well before the deadline established by the school/program.

5. Be prepared for the possibility that you'll have to interview (in person) with professors at one or more of the schools you've applied to. (Note: You can prepare for these interviews in much the same way you'd prepare for a job interview—see p. 224 if you need to refresh your memory.)

• ROAD MAP QUESTIONS •

Passions: Does your excitement for the discipline you hope to study come across in your graduate/professional school application? Will you stand out from the crowd?

_____

_____

_____

_____

Innate talents: Have you highlighted on your application your strongest abilities and skills? Will the admissions decision makers be able to see what you'll bring to their particular programs?

_____

_____

_____

_____

What matters most: Do your application materials—especially any essays you've written—effectively illustrate why it's so important for you to further your education in the discipline you hope to study?

_____

_____

_____

_____

The Personal Statement

Write a compelling *personal statement* to accompany your graduate/professional school application.

Why

Your *personal statement* serves as your "voice" in the initial graduate/professional school admission process. It introduces you to the selection committee and describes your most relevant experiences and what you've learned from them.

Make sure you write a compelling, grammatically sound statement that represents *you*. Be proud of it before you send it in!

How

1. Each of your graduate/professional school applications will require its own approach to developing a personal statement and/or answering any essay questions you might be asked. Read the questions carefully and make sure you answer them clearly. This advice might sound terribly obvious on the surface. But one of the biggest mistakes graduate/professional school applicants make is trying to use the same personal statement for each school they apply to instead of tweaking each one to address each school's/program's specific questions. It's typically very obvious to the selection committee who has taken the time to think about the school's/program's specific questions (and who has not).

2. Give yourself plenty of time to write your personal statement and answer any essay questions you're asked. This process will take a while and require some rewrites.

3. Show your personal statement to your academic advisor, faculty members who know you well, and others who can give you some expert feedback on it. Do they think your statement is compelling? And do they think your responses to any essay questions represent you accurately and positively?

• ROAD MAP QUESTIONS •

Passions: Does your passion for the academic work you'll be doing in a particular graduate/professional school program come across effectively in your personal statement? Have you clearly told the selection committee what you want to do with your graduate/professional degree and why?

_____

_____

_____

_____

Innate talents: Have you effectively highlighted the best you have to offer—your strongest abilities and skills—in your personal statement?

_____

_____

_____

What matters most: Will the selection committee get to know the real you through your personal statement?

_____

_____

_____

_____

Visiting Graduate/Professional School Campuses

Visit the campuses and interview professors and students at each institution to learn more about your top graduate/professional school choices.

Why

Choosing a graduate/professional school is a process that's similar to the one you probably went through when you chose your undergraduate institution. The stakes, however, are considerably higher.

You're looking for a program that matches your interests, your learning style, and your values. You need to figure out whether you connect with the faculty at a particular school and whether you feel comfortable there (especially since you'll be there several years!). You also need to determine whether you feel at home in the various communities you'll potentially be a part of—the community within your prospective academic department, the larger institutional community, and the surrounding local community.

How

1. Visiting campuses and interviewing people at those schools is a two-way process—you're judging and you're being judged. First impressions count. So be professional during the entire visiting and interviewing process, from how you contact the program to set up the visit to what you wear the day you arrive.

2. Prepare for your visits/interviews in two ways. First, just as you would for a job interview, use the STAR technique (see p. 209) to prepare stories illustrating your best abilities, skills, and experiences. Attending graduate/professional school is the "job" you want. Second, be sure to prepare (and write down) questions of your own to ask the professors, students, and staff members you meet during your visit.

3. Make sure each of your visits is comprehensive. Talk to faculty members and students; sit in on a class (or two or three); look at possible living arrangements; find out about research assistantships, fellowships, teaching assistantships, and scholarships; and visit with financial aid personnel.

4. Some graduate/professional school programs have very strict visit policies, so you may not have much control over your visit. If that's the

case, do the best you can to get your questions answered informally. You may need to rely on speaking to alumni/ae of the program to get your best information.

5. Collect contact information from everyone you meet on campus so that you can follow up with a thank-you note to each person immediately after you get home. It's common courtesy to thank people for their time and insights—and you'll stand out in doing so.

• ROAD MAP QUESTIONS •

Passions: Are you ready to speak succinctly about why a particular graduate/professional school and program are a good fit for you?

_____

_____

_____

_____

Innate talents: As you look around a particular campus and talk to various people there, do you think you'll be able to use your favorite abilities and skills—and learn new ones—during your time at the institution?

_____

_____

_____

_____

_____

What matters most: Can you see yourself pursuing your dreams at a particular school you've visited? Could it be your next home?

_____

_____

_____

_____

_____

_____

_____

_____

dreams … discoveries … reflections … intentions … discussions

——⊙——

Mapping Your Direction

Uncovering Your Purpose
Senior Year

*"What is happiness: to be dissolved into
something complete and great."*

~ WILLA CATHER

You're standing at the door to an incredible and exciting transition—your post-college life! How will you greet this transition and your changing world? What mark do you want to leave on the world in the years to come? What is your purpose and how will you live your life with that purpose?

These are the questions you'll want to ponder as you complete your senior year. If you can answer even a few of these questions, you'll go into The Real World with confidence and competence.

Purpose

How do you want to go into the world now that your undergraduate education will soon be complete? In what areas do you have unbridled confidence? What can you rely on in difficult times? What are your gifts?

_____

_____

_____

_____

_____

_____

_____

_____

_____

_____

_____

_____

_____

_____

_____

_____

_____

_____

Dreams—Life's Destinations

Where do you want to go at the end of your senior year? Do you want to live with a roommate, travel abroad, start a job, move home for a while? What will speak to the very core of your being as a young adult? How can you focus on the positive aspects of your upcoming transition and keep your mind from becoming fearful?

Discoveries

Scenic highways: What makes you feel totally alive and filled with excitement? As you leave this year behind, what do you want to take with you that has been a tremendously positive part of your life?

_____

_____

_____

_____

_____

_____

_____

_____

Roadblocks and speed bumps: What are you scared of or apprehensive about as you move out of your undergraduate years at college? How will you face these fears?

_____

_____

_____

_____

_____

_____

_____

_____

_____

Reflections

Have you discovered your own wisdom? Take at least ten minutes to write freely about what you have to offer the world with your personality, innate talents, skills, passions, and values. What makes you unique?

Intentions

Set your course: How will you examine your post-college world to make sure that what matters most to you is a central theme of your life? How will you be in the world that awaits you? Will you be reflective? open to learning? confident? quiet? observant? How will these intentions help you in being true to yourself?

_____

_____

_____

_____

_____

_____

_____

Daily intentions: What activities can you pursue each day of your senior year to best position yourself for your post-college life? How can you boost your confidence and reduce any apprehension you might have? Who can you turn to for help with these important tasks?

_____

_____

_____

_____

_____

_____

_____

_____

Discussion and Dialogue

Assessing your support system: Over these last few years, how has your relationship changed with the people who make up your support system?

Mapping Your Direction

Evaluate your senses, thoughts, feelings, and intuition right now. Do you have more clarity? What's still confusing to you? How can you cultivate and then maintain a healthy self-confidence? What do you need to do to get where you want to go?

The Best is Yet to Come

Congratulations! You've graduated from college—an achievement you've likely looked forward to with much anticipation.

Fascinating times lie ahead as you leave college for a future full of possibilities. By using *The College to Career Road Map* as a compass, you've established a foundation for living a life of purpose. Your world is ripe with opportunity. And even more exciting, you're now equipped with the skills you need to make wise choices—because you've already practiced how to make life decisions from the "inside out."

You'll be making career choices based on what you're passionate about, how you can best utilize your innate talents, and what matters most to you. The process of experiencing and reflecting outlined in *The College to Career Road Map* has helped you find your internal compass. You can now continue to practice this process as you make your way through life and follow the direction you know is best for you. Continue to listen to your heart, and to ask yourself the critical questions that challenge you to uncover your purpose.

We at College to Career, Inc. (www.collegetocareer.net) wish you well on your journey to reach your potential and fulfill your purpose. The possibilities are endless!

Kind regards!

~ Terese, Peter, and Judy

About the Authors

Terese Corey Blanck, M.Ed., offers unique expertise in college student development combined with in-depth knowledge of post-college business employment needs. For the past twenty years, Terese has worked closely with college students and recent graduates, helping them identify their innate talents and desires, plan their educational and career paths, and enhance both their personal development and career employability.

After receiving her Bachelor of Science degree in Elementary Education from Minnesota State University–Mankato and her Master of Education degree in College Student Development from Colorado State University, Terese spent the next twelve years working for small private universities as well as large public universities in the area of student affairs. She then joined the private sector, coaching college students and recent grads in career and life exploration.

Terese was inspired to launch College to Career, Inc. when she opened and managed the Minneapolis office of Grad Staff, Inc., a specialty-niche staffing firm that matches recent college graduates with employers such as Target, Wells Fargo Bank, and Best Buy. Through this work, she discovered that many recent graduates leave college not knowing what they want to do, much less having prepared themselves for the world of work. In response to this critical unmet need, Terese founded College to Career, Inc. to offer students a means for making decisions with direction during college—so they succeed after college.

A frequent speaker on college campuses, Terese also presents at major conferences on the topic of college student development. She has published numerous articles in the general market and lives in Minnesota with her husband and daughter.

Peter Vogt, M.S., is a career counselor, author, and speaker who encourages young adults to explore their many career possibilities and challenge the limiting beliefs, assumptions, and perceptions they often have about themselves and the world of work.

Peter devotes most of his time to writing and presenting for college students, college parents, and career practitioners across the United States. He's The MonsterTRAK Career Coach for leading global career web site Monster (www.monster.com); publisher of *Campus Career Counselor* (www.campuscareercounselor.com), a national newsletter for college/university career services professionals; and author of the book *Career Wisdom for College Students* (Facts On File, 2007). He's also been interviewed for articles in *Time* magazine, *U.S. News & World Report*, *The New York Times*, and many other media outlets.

Peter holds a master's degree in counseling from the University of Wisconsin–Whitewater and a bachelor's degree in mass communications from Minnesota State University–Moorhead. He lives in Minnesota with his wife and son.

Judith Anderson, M.A., has acquired a unique perspective working with college students and their parents at both large and small institutions throughout her entire professional career.

For the past twelve years, Judith has worked on college campuses in various roles in admissions, orientation and first-year programs, student leadership development, mentor programs, career services, residence life, and alumni relations. She has advised students in various student leadership roles, helping them discern and develop their innate talents, interests, and skills. Serving in these roles, she saw not only the importance of academic preparation, but more importantly experience, passion, and clarity for one's future endeavors.

Judith received her Bachelor of Arts degree in Political Science and Speech Communication from the University of Minnesota and holds a master's degree in Student Development in Higher Education from the University of Iowa. Most recently, she has served as a higher education consultant working both on campus and in the private sector. She has co-authored two handbooks for faculty members teaching first-year students at the University of Minnesota. As a partner with College to Career, Inc., Judy brings her campus experience and knowledge to parents and students, helping them make the most of their college experience. She lives in Minnesota with her husband and three children.

Judy Anderson, Peter Vogt, and Terese Corey Blanck